21ST Century
Communication 4

LISTENING, SPEAKING, AND CRITICAL THINKING

Second Edition

CHRISTIEN LEE

NATIONAL
GEOGRAPHIC
LEARNING

Australia · Brazil · Canada · Mexico · Singapore · United Kingdom · United States

National Geographic Learning,
a Cengage Company

21st Century Communication 4, Second Edition
Christien Lee

Publisher: Andrew Robinson

Executive Editor: Sean Bermingham

Senior Development Editor: Melissa Pang

Development Editors: Don Clyde Bhasy, Sophia Khan

Assistant Editor: Dawne Law

Director of Global Marketing: Ian Martin

Heads of Regional Marketing:

Charlotte Ellis (Europe, Middle East and Africa)

Justin Kaley (Asia and Greater China)

Irina Pereyra (Latin America)

Joy MacFarland (US and Canada)

Product Marketing Manager: Tracy Bailie

Senior Production Controller: Tan Jin Hock

Senior Media Researcher: Leila Hishmeh

Senior Designer: Heather Marshall

Operations Support: Hayley Chwazik-Gee

Manufacturing Buyer: Terrence Isabella

Composition: MPS North America LLC

For permission to use material from this text or product, submit all requests online at **cengage.com/permissions** Further permissions questions can be emailed to **permissionrequest@cengage.com**

Student's Book with Spark platform access:
ISBN-13: 978-0-357-85600-0

Student's Book:
ISBN-13: 978-0-357-86199-8

National Geographic Learning
200 Pier 4 Boulevard
Boston, MA 02210
USA

Locate your local office at **international.cengage.com/region**

Visit National Geographic Learning online at **ELTNGL.com**
Visit our corporate website at **www.cengage.com**

Printed in Mexico
Print Number: 01 Print Year: 2023

Topics and Featured Speakers

Scope and Sequence

Welcome to *21st Century Communication,* Second Edition

21st Century Communication Listening, Speaking, and Critical Thinking uses big ideas from TED and National Geographic to look at one topic from different perspectives, present real and effective communication models, and prepare students to share their ideas confidently in English. Each unit develops students' listening, speaking, and critical thinking skills to achieve their academic and personal goals.

A street sign in Stockholm, Sweden.

6
Hooked on Our Phones?

Q Do we use our phones too much?

Our phones are amazing devices, but do we use them too much? The street sign in the photo was put up by two Swedish artists precisely for that reason. Its purpose was to remind pedestrians to look up from their phones before crossing the street. In this unit, we'll explore the issues of phone usage and addiction, and consider whether smartphones are doing us more harm than good.

THINK and DISCUSS

1 Look at the photo and read the caption. Do you think the sign in the photo is effective? Why, or why not?

2 Look at the essential question and the unit introduction. How much do you use your phone? Do you think you're hooked on your phone?

Each unit opens with an **impactful photograph** to introduce the topic and act as a springboard for classroom discussion.

Q Do we use our phones too much?

Our phones are amazing devices, but do we use them too much? The street sign in the photo was put up by two Swedish artists precisely for that reason. Its purpose was to remind pedestrians to look up from their phones before crossing the street. In this unit, we'll explore the issues of phone usage and addiction, and consider whether smartphones are doing us more harm than good.

NEW The **Essential Question** outlines the central idea of the unit and directs students' focus to the main topic.

UPDATED **Building Vocabulary** uses infographics and readings to introduce vocabulary in context and teach words and phrases needed for academic studies.

Big ideas inspire many viewpoints. What's yours?

UPDATED **Viewing and Note-taking** allows students to explore one aspect of the unit theme and sharpen their academic skills with note-taking and listening comprehension practice.

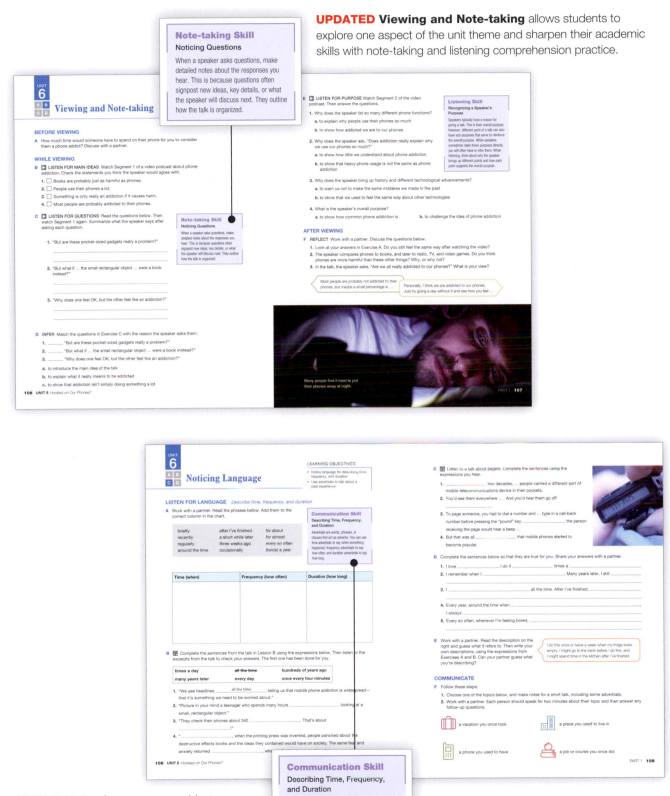

Note-taking Skill
Noticing Questions

When a speaker asks questions, make detailed notes about the responses you hear. This is because questions often signpost new ideas, key details, or what the speaker will discuss next. They outline how the talk is organized.

Communication Skill
Describing Time, Frequency, and Duration

Adverbials are words, phrases, or clauses that act as adverbs. You can use time adverbials to say *when* something happened, frequency adverbials to say *how often*, and duration adverbials to say *how long*.

NEW **Noticing Language** provides students with useful language structures and communication skills to share their ideas confidently.

NEW Communicating Ideas encourages students to express their opinions, make decisions, and explore solutions to problems through collaboration.

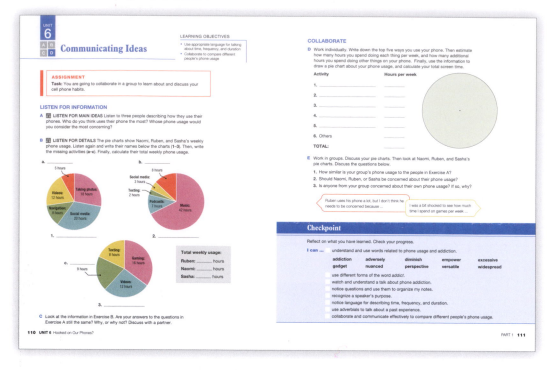

UPDATED Viewing and Note-taking uses big ideas from TED and National Geographic Explorers to present another aspect of the unit theme and help students improve their academic listening, note-taking skills, and pronunciation.

NEW Thinking Critically gives students a chance to synthesize, analyze, and evaluate the unit's ideas and find their voice in English.

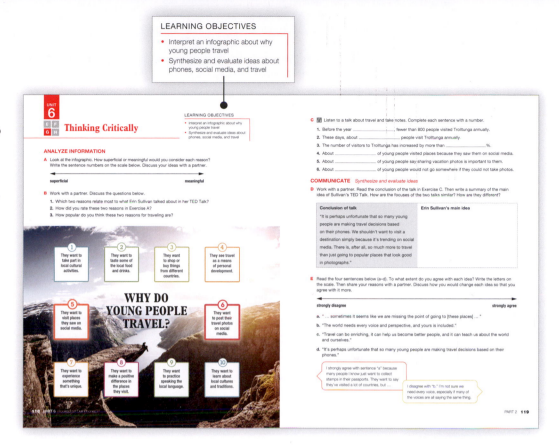

UPDATED Putting It Together has students prepare, plan, and present their ideas clearly and creatively in a final assignment.

The **Spark** platform delivers your digital tools for every stage of teaching and learning, including auto-graded Online Practice activities, customizable Assessment Suite tests and quizzes, Student's eBook, Classroom Presentation Tool, and downloadable Teacher's Resources.

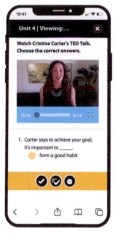

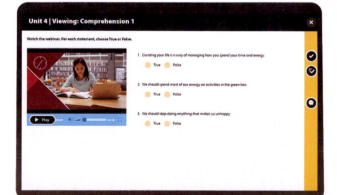

Pedestrians surrounded by media messages in Times Square in New York, U.S.A.

1

Reality Check

Q **Can we trust the media?**

The photo shows Times Square, New York, lined with giant advertisements and flashing news headlines. There's no escape from the media for these pedestrians, and the same can be said for most of us. Every day, we are bombarded by so many media messages that it has become more important than ever for us to be able to distinguish between trustworthy and unreliable information. In this unit, we'll examine how and why the media sometimes distorts the truth, and explore strategies for coping with all of this information.

THINK and DISCUSS

1 Look at the photo and read the caption. How do you think the media influences you?

2 Look at the essential question and the unit introduction. How much do you trust the media?

Building Vocabulary

LEARNING OBJECTIVES

• Use ten words related to news media
• Use collocations with *media*

LEARN KEY WORDS

A Listen to and read the information below. What are some "soft news" stories you have read in the past? Discuss with a partner.

Is Soft News Really News?

When we think about the news, we usually think about war, natural disasters, or important topics like science, politics, and business. But news stories aren't always serious. Every now and then, we get a heartwarming **anecdote** about an adorable dog or cat, or some **sensational** story about a famous celebrity misbehaving.

In the world of **journalism**, news like this is called "soft news." Soft news is a broad term, but its defining trait is that it is usually more for enjoyment or entertainment. Many people feel the quality of news is declining, and that soft news is partly to blame. So why then does soft news still exist in our **media**? The easy answer is that it sells. People like feel-good articles and juicy celebrity stories.

But for some people, soft news isn't actually soft. Sports **coverage**, for example, is more than just entertainment to people who actually work in sports. Also, imagine how anxious we'd all be if all our news stories were serious or heavy. Some feel that it's irresponsible to place **disproportionate** emphasis on bad news. Soft news is important because it reminds us that positive and fun things happen, too.

So is soft news really news, or just pointless entertainment? It probably depends on who you ask.

Sugar the surf dog takes part in a surf contest at Huntington Beach, California, U.S.A.

	HARD NEWS	SOFT NEWS
CHARACTERISTICS	• Important • Current and time-sensitive • Informative and objective	• Entertaining • Not as time-sensitive • Appeals to emotions
COMMON TOPICS	• Local and international events • Politics • Business and economics • Health and medicine • Education	• Entertainment or celebrity news • Lifestyle news • Arts and culture • Sports • Feel-good pieces

B Match each word in **bold** from Exercise A with its meaning.

1. _____ anecdote
2. _____ media
3. _____ journalism
4. _____ coverage
5. _____ sensational
6. _____ disproportionate

a. the work of writing, publishing or broadcasting news
b. shocking or exciting
c. significantly more or less than is required
d. a personal story
e. TV, print, radio, and the internet
f. the reporting of a particular news story or event

C Read the passage. Then complete the sentences with the correct form of the words in **bold**.

Statistics show that many news agencies fail every year. To survive, some smaller agencies turn to tabloid journalism. Tabloid journalism focuses on stories that are sensational. These can be fun, but many are **negligent**: they ignore facts and report gossip to increase **subscriptions**. To many, tabloid journalism is harmful. It **distorts** the truth and distracts us from what's important.

1. The fees people pay to get access to media products are called _____.

2. To be careless or irresponsible is to be _____.

3. Numerical data that people use to show patterns or trends are called _____.

4. If you manipulate facts to create a misleading or false impression, you _____ them.

D The words in the box collocate with the noun **media**. Complete the sentences using the correct words.

coverage	literacy	frenzy	industry

1. There was a media _____ when the singer announced her surprise concert.

2. With so much news out there, we need to start teaching media _____ in school.

3. The media _____ is made up of many different types of companies.

4. The press release was a success. The media _____ they got was amazing.

COMMUNICATE

E Work with a partner. Discuss a few examples for each prompt.

1. something that caused a **media frenzy**
2. a media service that requires a **subscription**
3. a news story that received **disproportionate coverage**

F Work with a partner. Discuss the questions below.

1. Do you think that soft news is important and necessary? Why, or why not?
2. Do you believe that tabloid journalism is harmful to people? Why, or why not?

Viewing and Note-taking

LEARNING OBJECTIVES

- Watch a class discussion about fear in the media
- Use abbreviations for numerical information
- Recognize repetition of important details

BEFORE VIEWING

A Look at the abbreviations in the box below. Which ones do you already use? What other abbreviations for numerical information do you know? Discuss with a partner.

Percentages	25%	"25 percent of"
Fractions	⅓	"a third of"
Thousands	4.5k cars	"four thousand five hundred cars"
Millions	2M homes	"two million homes"
More than	> 30%	"over 30%"
Less than	< 60%	"under 60%"
Estimates	~ $3M	"about three million dollars"

> **Note-taking Skill**
> **Using Abbreviations for Numerical Information**
>
> When noting down numerical information, it's often quicker and more accurate to use abbreviations. There are many common abbreviations you can use. You can also create your own abbreviations.

B 🎧 Listen to a talk about how people get their news. Note the numerical information you hear using the abbreviations above.

Digital news sources	Non-digital news sources

C Use your notes in Exercise B to answer these questions.

1. _____ two thirds of U.S. adults get their news from websites and apps. That's about _____ people.

2. _____ half of U.S. adults get their news from social media.

3. _____ one fifth of U.S. adults get their news from podcasts.

4. Just over _____ of U.S. adults, or _____ percent, get their news from TV.

5. Seven _____ of U.S. adults get their news from radio.

6. Only _____ in _____ people get their news from print sources.

WHILE VIEWING

D ▶ **LISTEN FOR MAIN IDEAS** Watch Segment 1 of a class discussion. For each opinion below, check (✓) whether it is voiced by Matteo or Lina, or both of them.

	Matteo	Lina
1. There are more fear-based stories in the media than before.	☐	☐
2. The world is becoming more dangerous.	☐	☐
3. The environment is getting worse.	☐	☐
4. Frightening news stories are more interesting to readers.	☐	☐
5. News companies need to make money.	☐	☐

E ▶ **LISTEN FOR DETAILS** Watch Segment 2 of the class discussion. Circle **T** for true or **F** for false.

1. Murder coverage increased because murder rates went up.	T	F
2. Bullying is less of a problem now than it was a few decades ago.	T	F
3. Murder rates in about 75% of the world have gone down.	T	F
4. Thea's sister believes the news stories she hears about the city.	T	F
5. Thea believes most people think critically about the news.	T	F

F ▶ **RECOGNIZE REPETITION** Watch an excerpt from the class discussion. Discuss with a partner.

1. How many times does Matteo mention that the world is getting worse?

2. Why do you think he repeats this point?

> **Listening Skill**
> **Recognizing Repetition**
>
> Speakers usually repeat important ideas. They often paraphrase when they repeat; they rarely use the exact same words. Sometimes, speakers will signpost the repeated idea using phrases like *as mentioned* or *as I said*.

AFTER VIEWING

G **EVALUATE** Complete the tasks below.

1. Work individually and complete the chart. Why is the news getting scarier? Summarize Matteo's and Lina's positions, then add your own. Who do you agree with more? Why?

2. Work with a partner. Discuss Matteo's and Lina's views and share your own. Use the chart to help you.

Matteo	Lina	You

Noticing Language

LISTEN FOR LANGUAGE *Ask rhetorical questions*

A Read the expressions below. Which two expressions signal that you've already considered an obvious question that's probably on a lot of people's minds? Discuss with a partner.

What does that really mean?	Why's that?
Don't you wish … ?	Aren't you glad … ?
Who really wants … ?	Who wouldn't want … ?
… , isn't it?	… , don't you?
You must be wondering: … ?	I know what you're thinking: … ?

> **Communication Skill**
> **Asking Rhetorical Questions**
>
> A question is rhetorical if it doesn't require an answer. Speakers sometimes ask rhetorical questions to guide listeners' thoughts through complex topics. They also ask (and answer) them when the information they've presented raises an obvious question, to show they've considered what's on everyone's mind.

B 🎧 Listen to five excerpts from the class discussion in Lesson B. Check (✓) the three excerpts containing questions that are rhetorical.

1. ☐ Excerpt 1   **4.** ☐ Excerpt 4

2. ☐ Excerpt 2   **5.** ☐ Excerpt 5

3. ☐ Excerpt 3

C 🎧 Listen to the three rhetorical questions from Exercise B. Match the questions to the reasons for asking them.

a. _____ to show awareness of a question people may have

b. _____ to get people thinking about the topic

c. _____ to reinforce a point by making it more relatable

D Complete the sentences. Use appropriate expressions from the box above.

1. _____: why would a young person like me choose to get her news from the radio?

2. So you probably think I get all my news online, _____?

3. _____ you could spend more time away from screens sometimes?

4. I used to watch TV news a lot, but not anymore. _____? Well …

5. I mean, _____ to listen to that much news?

According to a 2022 U.S. survey, 55% of people aged 18–34 still like to read a newspaper from time to time.

E 🎧 Listen to three people talking about their favorite news sources. Did they use the same expressions you used in Exercise D?

COMMUNICATE

F How do you get your news? Note in the chart below why you like or don't like each way of getting news.

News websites and apps	TV news channels	Newspapers and magazines	Radio news stations	Social media platforms

G Work in a group. Take it in turns to give a short talk about where you like to get your news. Use rhetorical questions when explaining your preferences and to raise obvious questions that need answering.

> I think TV news channels are biased. What does that mean? Well, …

Communicating Ideas

LEARNING OBJECTIVES

• Use appropriate language for asking rhetorical questions
• Collaborate to prioritize different news stories

ASSIGNMENT

Task: You are going to collaborate in a group to decide which news stories should feature on a news website's homepage.

LISTEN FOR INFORMATION

A 🎧 **LISTEN FOR MAIN IDEAS** Listen to a conversation between two newspaper editors. What three news stories are they considering using as their headline? Write brief notes below.

1. Story 1: _____

2. Story 2: _____

3. Story 3: _____

B 🎧 **LISTEN FOR DETAILS** Listen again and complete the chart. Summarize the pros and cons of each story.

Story	Pros	Cons

C Work with a partner. Which of the three stories do you think should lead, and why? Why not the others?

COLLABORATE

D Work in a group. You are a team of editors for an online news website. Think of ten headlines that are attention grabbing. Use your imagination—the stories don't have to be real. Cover a range of different topics.

> How about *Local College Student Wins National Science Contest*?

> Sure, that's a nice human-interest story. And how about …

E In groups, rank your headlines from 1 (most important) to 10 (least important). Rank them again from 1 (most interesting) to 10 (least interesting). Then, decide which five headlines to feature on the homepage of your news site. Write one headline in each of the five boxes below, based on how important and interesting you think the stories are.

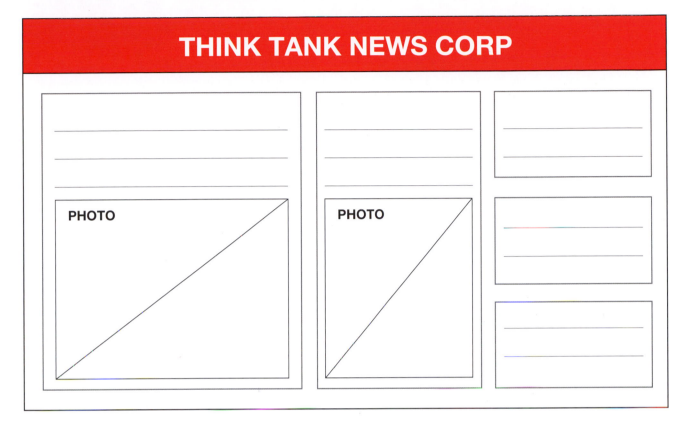

F Work with a partner from a different group. Discuss your homepages in Exercise E. Which stories would you be most interested in reading? Would you prioritize your partner's stories differently?

Checkpoint

Reflect on what you have learned. Check your progress.

I can ...   understand and use words related to news media.

anecdote	**coverage**	**disproportionate**	**distort**	**journalism**
media	**negligent**	**sensational**	**statistic**	**subscription**

     use collocations with the word *media*.

     watch and understand a class discussion about fear in the media.

     use abbreviations to note numerical information.

     listen for the repetition of important details.

     notice language for asking rhetorical questions.

     use rhetorical questions in a talk about preferred news sources.

     collaborate and communicate effectively to prioritize different news stories.

A fake photo from 1894 of a man holding a giant potato.

MAGGIE MURPHY POTATO
WEIGHT. 86 LBS. 10 OZ.
TOO LARGE TO EAT — ONLY FIT FOR SEED !
For Particulars of This and 200 Other Varieties Write the Grower.
J. B. SWAN, LOVELAND, COLO

Building Vocabulary

LEARN KEY WORDS

A 🎧 Listen to and read the passage below. Why are fake photos a big problem today? Discuss with a partner.

Fake Photos

Photographs have the power to **shape** what we believe. And some even change the world, like the "Blue Marble" photo of Earth in 1972, which helped start the environmental movement. It's therefore no surprise that **fake** photos have existed for nearly two centuries.

In the early days of photography, creating a fake photo wasn't easy. People had to physically combine elements from different images and paint the parts they wanted to change by hand. Despite this, many fake photos from this period were still very convincing and almost impossible to spot.

Digital photography changed everything. Today, with the help of computers, people can manipulate photos in any way imaginable. Magazines and websites feature photos of celebrities with their features **enhanced** and flaws removed. And doctoring a photo is so easy that anybody can do it with just a little practice.

Photo editing technology isn't all bad. It opens up new possibilities in business, art, and science. But as fake photos become easier to create and harder to **detect**, the risk they pose becomes bigger. News stories that **misrepresent** reality are more convincing than ever because the fake photos they're based on look so real.

B Work with a partner. Discuss the questions below.

1. Do you know how to doctor an image or create a fake photo?

2. Look at the photo and caption. How do you think this photo was made? Is it still convincing by today's standards?

C Match the correct form of each word in **bold** from Exercise A with its meaning.

1. _____ not real, or not the original version

2. _____ to spot or identify

3. _____ to influence and change someone or something

4. _____ to describe in a way that isn't true

5. _____ to improve the quality of something

D Read the excerpts from Supasorn Suwajanakorn's TED Talk in Lesson F. Circle the options that are closest in meaning to the words in **bold**.

1. "Then we synthesize the texture, enhance details and teeth, and blend it into the head and background from a **source** video."

   a. a new version of something

   b. where something comes from

2. " … fake videos could do a lot of damage, even before anyone has a chance to **verify**, so it's very important that we make everyone aware … "

   a. check if something is true

   b. decide what to do with something

3. "Our goal was to build an accurate model of a person … but one thing that concerns me is its potential for **misuse**."

   a. being utilized in a way that's wrong

   b. being utilized without permission

4. " … we actually teach the computer to **imitate** the way someone talks …"

   a. change

   b. copy

5. " ... so next, we develop a new blending technique that improves upon ... facial **textures** and colors."

   a. the roughness or smoothness of a surface

   b. the sharpness or blurriness of an image

E Complete the chart below with the correct words. Use a dictionary to help you if necessary.

Noun	Verb
	detect
	misrepresent
misuse	
	verify

COMMUNICATE

F Work with a partner. Think of two additional examples of things that can:

1. be detected   light

2. be fake   a photo

3. be enhanced   a flavor

4. blend together   smells

G Work in a group. Share two of the examples you wrote in Exercise F, but don't say what the prompt is. Your classmates have to guess. Discuss your examples and explain why you chose them.

My examples are *chemicals* and *life on other planets*. What am I talking about?

Things that can be detected?

Viewing and Note-taking

LEARNING OBJECTIVES

- Watch and understand a talk about fake videos
- Organize words into thought groups

TEDTALKS

Supasorn Suwajanakorn is an award-winning scientist who specializes in machine learning and computer vision. In his TED Talk, *Fake Videos of Real People—and How to Spot Them*, he discusses a technology he helped create, and its potential for misuse.

BEFORE VIEWING

A Read the information about Supasorn Suwajanakorn. Work with a partner and discuss the questions below.

1. What are some possible benefits of making fake videos of real people?
2. What problems could producing fake videos of real people cause?

> **"** I think these results seem very realistic and intriguing, but at the same time frightening, even to me. **"**

Daniel Craig

Hillary Clinton

Ian M

Barack Obama

Piers Morgan

To

Source: Published July 7, 2013, George W. Bush, Laura Bush 'This Week

B ▶ **LISTEN FOR MAIN IDEAS** Watch Segment 1 of Supasorn Suwajanakorn's TED Talk. Note down what he says about his creation in the chart below.

1. What did he create?	2. What inspired him?

3. How can it be used?	4. How does it work?

C ▶ **LISTEN FOR DETAILS** Refer to your notes in Exercise B and check (✓) two answers for each question. Watch Segment 1 again to check your answers.

1. In his talk, Suwajanakorn mentions creating his face-swapping technology so that ...

   a. ☐ people can learn from historical figures who are no longer alive.

   b. ☐ computer-generated "bots" can behave in more human-like ways.

   c. ☐ people can get advice from relatives who are no longer with them.

   d. ☐ people can produce movies without needing actual actors.

2. How does Suwajanakorn's technology work?

   a. ☐ An algorithm analyzes a large number of photos.

   b. ☐ A 3D model is photographed from different angles.

   c. ☐ A camera pre-records a person's different expressions.

   d. ☐ A special blending technique enhances colors and details.

WORDS IN THE TALK
hologram (n) a special type of 3D image
algorithm (n) a mathematical rule used by computer programs
countermeasure (n) a strategy to avoid or deal with a problem

D ▶ **LISTEN FOR DETAILS** Watch Segment 2 of the TED Talk. Circle **T** for true or **F** for false.

1. Suwajanakorn isn't worried about people misusing his technology. **T** **F**
2. Reality Defender helps people detect fake videos online. **T** **F**
3. Suwajanakorn believes people need to be aware of what technology like his can do. **T** **F**
4. Suwajanakorn thinks creating his technology was a mistake. **T** **F**

AFTER VIEWING

E **APPLY** Work with a partner. Discuss the positive and negative uses of Suwajanakorn's technology. Complete the chart below as fully as possible.

Positive uses	Negative uses

F **EVALUATE** Look at your chart. Do you feel the advantages of his technology outweigh the disadvantages? Why, or why not?

PRONUNCIATION   *Organize words into thought groups*

G 🎧 Read the options below. Which one divides the sentence into thought groups most naturally? Listen and check.

> **Pronunciation Skill**
>
> **Organizing Words into Thought Groups**
>
> Sentences can be divided into thought groups, with each group of words expressing an idea. Speakers usually pause between thought groups and stress the final content word.

  a. "So it's very / important that we make everyone / aware of what's currently / possible so we can have the right / assumption and be critical about what we see."

  b. "So it's very important / that we make everyone aware / of what's currently possible / so we can have the right assumption / and be critical about what we see."

  c. "So it's very important that / we make everyone aware of / what's currently possible so / we can have the right assumption and / be critical about what we see."

H Look again at the introduction of Suwajanakorn from the beginning of Lesson F. Divide the sentences into natural thought groups. Then practice reading the sentences aloud to a partner. Give each other feedback.

> Supasorn Suwajanakorn is an award-winning scientist who specializes in machine learning and computer vision. In his TED Talk, *Fake Videos of Real People — and How to Spot Them,* he discusses a technology he helped create, and its potential for misuse.

Thinking Critically

ANALYZE INFORMATION

A Read the news article in the infographic and answer the questions. Discuss your answers with a partner.

1. What do you know about fluoride in tap water?

2. Do you think this article can be trusted?

B 🎧 Look at the rest of the infographic and listen to a talk about spotting false or fake content online. Discuss the questions with a partner.

1. What is the difference between misinformation and disinformation?

2. What does *biases* in point 7 mean?

3. Which point do you feel is the most important?

Is It Real?

1. Check the URL.
- *Does it match the site?*
- *What country does it belong to?*

2. Consider who owns the site.

3. Investigate the author.

4. Evaluate the text.

5. Evaluate other information.

6. Evaluate the sources.

7. Check your own biases.

http://sjc_scanhack_13471/giro.com.co

REAL DEAL NEWS
Everything they don't want you to know.

Fluoride in Water at All Time High
by Jason "the Bulldog" Walker

Official sources are saying that fluoride levels in our tap water is higher than ever! Not concerned? You should be! Check out our video about the negative effects of fluoride on your brain.

Real Deal has been protesting this issue on you're behalf for years! So why then is nothing been done?!? I wrote an email last week, and they're reply was vague and rude. How typical of our government!

C 🎧 Listen to the talk again. For each point, write one or two short questions you can ask yourself to help you spot fake or false content. Box 1 has been completed for you.

D Read the article in the infographic again. Circle examples of things that show it is not trustworthy. Use the seven tips in the infographic to help you.

E Work with a partner. Look at what you circled in Exercise D. Then read the statements below. Do you agree? Circle **Y** (yes), **N** (no), or **U** (unsure).

1.	The website's URL looks safe.	Y	N	U
2.	The article's headline isn't sensational.	Y	N	U
3.	The article's author is reputable.	Y	N	U
4.	The sources listed are reliable.	Y	N	U
5.	The tone of the article is neutral.	Y	N	U
6.	There are no spelling or grammar errors.	Y	N	U
7.	My biases aren't affecting my reading of the article.	Y	N	U

COMMUNICATE   *Synthesize and evaluate ideas*

F Work in a group. Discuss the questions below, using ideas from the infographic and Suwajanakorn's TED Talk in Lesson F.

1. Which tip(s) could apply to the types of videos described in the TED Talk? What does the speaker in Exercise B suggest we do for videos like these?

2. What are some other tips that can help you determine if the information in a video or website is reliable?

G Work in a group. Read the two quotations from the TED Talk in Lesson F. Then answer the questions. Give reasons for your answers.

> " ... it's very important that we make everyone aware of what's currently possible so we can have the right assumption and be critical about what we see."
>
> "There's still a long way to go before we can fully model individual people and before we can ensure the safety of this technology."

1. Do you think most people know how easy it is to produce fake content?

2. Are most people aware that there's a lot of fake content online?

3. Are people generally able to recognize fake content?

4. Will it ever be possible to ensure the safety of technology like Suwajanakorn's?

I think most people know that fake content is a problem, but …

I think technology like that will only be safe if …

Putting It Together

LEARNING OBJECTIVES

- Research, plan, and present on the reliability of a news source
- Start a presentation with an interesting or challenging question

ASSIGNMENT

Individual presentation: You are going to give a presentation about how your classmates feel regarding the reliability of the news we get from a certain source.

PREPARE

A Review the unit. List a few general news sources, such as newspapers or websites. Then list a few reasons why news stories are sometimes unreliable.

General news sources	Things that make news unreliable

B Work with a partner. Choose one of your news sources in Exercise A. Then read the survey question below. Use your notes above to write three more questions about the reliability of news from that source. Make sure the questions can be answered on a scale from 1 to 10.

News source: _____

1. How trustworthy is the news from this source?   1 2 3 4 5 6 7 8 9 10
2. _____   1 2 3 4 5 6 7 8 9 10
3. _____   1 2 3 4 5 6 7 8 9 10
4. _____   1 2 3 4 5 6 7 8 9 10

C Plan your presentation. Ask three classmates your questions in Exercise B and record their answers. Ask follow-up questions and include any useful information in the comments column. Use the information in the chart to arrive at a meaningful conclusion.

	S1	S1	S3	Comments
Q1				
Q2				
Q3				
Q4				

D Look back at the vocabulary, pronunciation, and communication skills you've learned in this unit. What can you use in your presentation? Note any useful language below.

_____

_____

_____

E Search online for surprising or interesting information related to your presentation. Then prepare a question to ask at the start of your presentation that your audience will find engaging.

_____

_____

_____

Presentation Skill

Starting With a Question

Starting a presentation with an interesting, tricky, or challenging question is a great way to engage listeners early. Supasorn Suwajanakorn does this to great effect at the start of his own TED Talk. You can do the same for your presentation, too.

F Practice your presentation. Make use of the presentation skill that you've learned.

PRESENT

G Give your presentation to a partner. Watch their presentation and evaluate them using the Presentation Scoring Rubrics at the back of the book.

H Discuss your evaluation with your partner. Give feedback on two things they did well and two areas for improvement.

Checkpoint

Reflect on what you have learned. Check your progress.

I can ... ☐ understand and use words to talk about fake images.

detect	enhance	fake	imitate	misrepresent
misuse	shape	source	texture	verify

☐ use different forms of _detect, misrepresent, misuse,_ and _verify._

☐ watch and understand a talk about fake videos.

☐ organize words into thought groups.

☐ interpret an infographic about how to recognize fake content online.

☐ synthesize and evaluate ideas about different kinds of false information.

☐ start a presentation with an interesting or challenging question.

☐ give a presentation on the reliability of a news source.

Hundreds of practitioners form a yoga circle at the foot of the Eiffel Tower, in Paris, France.

2

Self Therapy

Q ### How much do our habits affect who we are?

Who are we? For some, we are what we believe or value, but for others, we are defined more by what we do. Is it therefore possible to change who we are by changing our actions? In the photo, yoga practitioners from around the world have come together at the Eiffel Tower to celebrate International Yoga Day. Yoga is widely regarded as an effective way to cultivate our own mental and physical well-being, but there are many other things we can do to shape who we are. In this unit, we'll consider some of these methods, and explore both the potential and the limitations of self therapy.

THINK and DISCUSS

1 Look at the photo and read the caption. What are the people doing? What might be the benefits of this activity?

2 Look at the essential question and the unit introduction. Do you think we can change who we are by changing what we do? Why, or why not?

Building Vocabulary

LEARN KEY WORDS

A 🎧 Listen to and read the information below. Which of the habits do you already have? How did you develop these habits?

The Life-Changing Power of Habits

Sit up straight. Tidy up your room. And stop biting your nails! Parents and teachers everywhere seem to be quite aware of just how important it is to **adopt** good habits and break bad ones. Habits are powerful things, and we've known this for a long time.

Writer Will Durant once famously paraphrased the Greek philosopher Aristotle: "We are what we repeatedly do. Excellence, then, is not an act, but a habit." Many successful people are aware of this and try to **incorporate** good habits into their lives. To avoid feeling **fatigued**, they eat well, exercise often, and get enough sleep. They also make other **adjustments** that improve their efficiency and reduce wasted time.

So why don't more people **modify** their lives this way? One well-known experiment showed that most people had to **persevere** for about two months in order to make a simple habit automatic. And while some people required less time, others never even succeeded during the eight-month-long experiment. Similar timeframes apply to breaking existing habits, which research suggests isn't much different than forming new ones. For most of us, changing our habits requires a little determination!

HABITS YOU CAN COUNT ON

Get off your chair and move around more.

Limit your non-essential screen time.

Laugh more to reduce stress.

Drink plenty of water.

Go outside for regular walks.

Read to learn, and read for fun.

Get enough sleep every night.

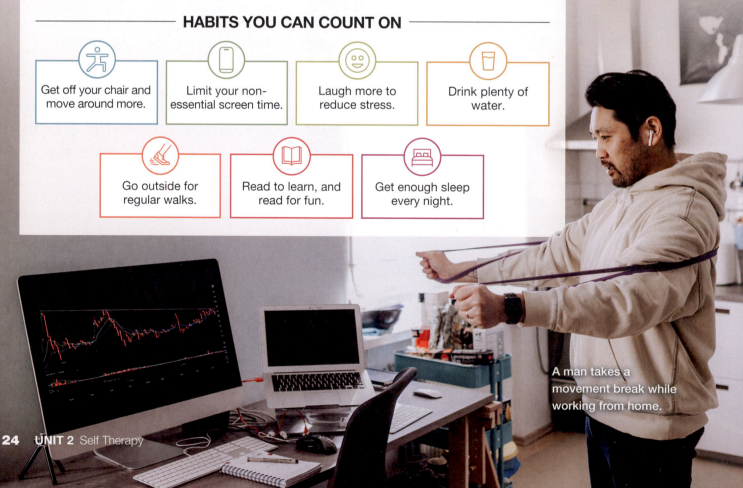

A man takes a movement break while working from home.

B Complete the definitions below using the words in **bold** from Exercise A.

1. _____ are small changes that you make to something.

2. If you _____ , you keep doing something even though it's difficult.

3. When you make something part of a larger whole, you _____ it.

4. You _____ something by making changes to it.

5. To _____ a new idea or practice is to try something new.

6. Someone who is _____ feels tired.

C Read the passage below. Then match the words in **bold** to their definitions.

Can't get rid of a bad habit? **Swap** it for a better one. Breaking a habit takes **discipline**, but it's easier when there's something to replace it with. Imagine trying to eat fewer sugary snacks. Changing how you snack is a much smaller **lifestyle** change than not snacking at all, so try some almonds instead. **Consistency** is key, though. Doing it once is not enough. You have to do it over and over again.

1. _____ swap   **a.** the ability to stay in control of one's behavior

2. _____ discipline   **b.** being the same over a period of time

3. _____ lifestyle   **c.** replace something with another thing

4. _____ consistency   **d.** a person's usual way of living

D Complete the sentences. Circle the correct form of each word.

1. It's a long, tough race, so **persevere / perseverance** is key.

2. The **modify / modifications** were small, but they made a big difference.

3. He's finding it hard to **adjust / adjustment** to city life.

4. The **adopt / adoption** of the policy had a big effect on the town.

E Complete the passage. Use the words in **bold** from Exercises A and C.

My current ¹_____ isn't great. I don't exercise much, I'm stuck to my computer all day, and I feel ²_____ all the time. It's time for a change! I think I'll start few small ³_____. I'll set my alarm, and every hour, I'll take a 15-minute standing break. I'll ⁴_____ my short desk for the high table in the pantry where I can work while standing. It won't be easy. I'll need to ⁵_____ !

COMMUNICATE

F Work with a partner. Discuss the questions below.

1. Look back at the infographic. What are some other habits that could make your life better?

2. Have you recently tried to adopt any new habits? What were they, and did you succeed?

3. What are some good ways to pick up a new habit, or to break an old one?

Viewing and Note-taking

LEARNING OBJECTIVES

- Watch a video podcast about improving your life
- Use visuals to guide note-taking
- Listen for supporting evidence

BEFORE VIEWING

A Work with a partner. What are some things people usually upgrade? Do you think it's possible to "upgrade" your life? If so, how?

WHILE VIEWING

B ▶ **LISTEN FOR MAIN IDEAS** Watch a video podcast about upgrading your life. Take notes. Use the outline below.

TITLE: [1]_____

- Replace parts that [2]_____.
- Add parts that [3]_____.

ONE SIMPLE EXAMPLE:

[4]_____.

WHY?

- Enjoy noticeable [5]_____.
- Experience [6]_____ loss.

BETA-LEVEL UPGRADE:

- Walk in [7]_____: double your rewards.
- Enjoy physical and [8]_____ benefits.

HARDER THAN IT SEEMS:

- [9]_____ is tricky: requires discipline.
- Consider making a few simple [10]_____.

> **Note-taking Skill**
>
> **Using Visuals to Guide Note-taking**
>
> Speakers often organize their main ideas and key details clearly in their visuals, so make use of them to help you organize your own notes. Visuals can also contain information that the speaker doesn't verbally mention, so look out for such information when watching a talk.

C ▶ **LISTEN FOR DETAILS** Watch again. Check (✓) the ideas the speaker expresses.

1. ☐ It's possible to swap our lives for better ones.

2. ☐ Walking helps prevent and manage some serious health conditions.

3. ☐ Walking is good for you, no matter where you do it.

4. ☐ Walking every day for 30 minutes sounds easy, but isn't.

5. ☐ Life upgrades often require us to spend a little money.

D ▶ **LISTEN FOR SUPPORTING EVIDENCE** Watch an excerpt from the video podcast. Then complete the notes below.

JAPAN STUDY:

When did it happen? What does it tell us?

1 _____

_____

MIKE EVANS'S 23½ HOURS:

Who is Mike Evans? What does his lecture tell us?

2 _____

_____

STEVEN BLAIR'S STUDY:

Who is Steven Blair? What does his study tell us?

3 _____

_____

THE WORK OF DAVID SUZUKI:

Who is David Suzuki? What does his work tell us?

4 _____

_____

AFTER VIEWING

E **REFLECT** What do you think about the benefits of walking every day for 30 minutes? Would you be willing to modify your lifestyle in order to gain these benefits? Why, or why not? Discuss with a partner.

> The benefits are great, but I can't walk every day. I have too much to do already.

> I wonder if there are some ways you can make small changes to get a walk in …

A rambler enjoys a walk in Mount Seymour Provincial Park, Vancouver, Canada.

Noticing Language

LISTEN FOR LANGUAGE *Start with your selling points*

A Read the expressions below. When might you use expressions like these? Discuss with a partner.

What if … ?	What if I told you … ?
Imagine …	Picture yourself …
How would you feel if … ?	Wouldn't that be amazing?
You'd be interested, wouldn't you?	So what's the secret?

> **Communication Skill**
> **Starting With Selling Points**
>
> Sometimes, in order to make a suggestion more appealing, it helps to list all the benefits first before explaining how to get them. This is a strategy that's often used in marketing and advertising.

B 🎧 Listen to an excerpt from the video podcast in Lesson B. Answer the questions. Then compare answers with a partner.

1. Which expressions from the gray box above does the speaker use? Circle the expressions you hear.

2. What type of benefits does the speaker use as selling points? How do we get to enjoy these benefits?

_____

_____

3. Does the speaker mention the selling points before or after making her suggestion?

_____

_____

4. Would the speaker's suggestion seem more or less attractive if she switched the order? Why?

_____

_____

C 🎧 Complete the sentences from advertisements using words from the gray box in Exercise A. Then listen to the advertisements and check your answers.

1. Tired of your slow internet connection? _____ having the fastest download speeds in town at only half the cost!

2. Too much responsibility at work and at home? _____ would you feel if you finally had the time and energy to do the things you want to do?

3. Picture _____ sitting on a beach. The air is warm, the sea is blue, and your worries are an ocean away. _____ that be amazing?

4. What if I _____ you that you could improve your sleep and wake up refreshed every morning with one simple lifestyle change? You'd be _____, wouldn't you? So what's the _____?

COMMUNICATE

D Work with a partner. Prepare to convince your friends to adopt the three habits below. Write one possible selling point for each habit.

1. Practice yoga every morning

Imagine _____

_____

2. Spend less money every month

What if _____

_____

3. Do volunteer work regularly

Picture yourself _____

_____

E Work with a new partner. Present your selling points before saying what they'd need to do to enjoy them. Discuss how appealing your selling points were, and ways to improve your approach.

F Follow the steps below.

1. Work with a new partner. Tell each other about a habit you want to break. Take notes.

2. Work individually. Think of a suggestion that would help your partner break their habit. Think of the benefits of following that suggestion as well. Take notes.

3. Work with your partner again. Persuade them to adopt your suggestion. Start with the benefits before explaining what they have to do.

> So, you told me earlier that you wished you didn't use your phone so much because it distracts you. Well, what if you had something more interesting with you? Something that didn't distract you, but that made you pay attention? Try carrying an actual camera with you …

Communicating Ideas

A B
C D

LEARNING OBJECTIVES

- Use appropriate language for listing selling points
- Collaborate to persuade someone to start using a product

ASSIGNMENT

Task: You are going to collaborate with a partner to try to convince a classmate to start using a product that would help upgrade their life.

LISTEN FOR INFORMATION

A 🎧 **LISTEN FOR MAIN IDEAS** Listen to someone talking about their fitness tracker watch. What does the speaker say? Circle the answers.

1. The speaker thinks her fitness tracker watch is like _____.

   a. an exercise buddy   **b.** a fitness trainer

2. The feature the speaker uses most often is _____.

   a. the reminder function   **b.** the sleep tracker

3. The fitness tracker makes exercise more interesting by _____.

   a. recommending different   **b.** tracking how much you
   workouts   walk and run

4. The feature the speaker appreciates most is the _____.

   a. activity-monitoring feature   **b.** sleep-monitoring feature

B 🎧 **LISTEN FOR DETAILS** Listen again. Complete the notes below with information from the talk.

Cost: ¹_____

Sensor tells you:

- when you haven't ²_____.
- how much you ³_____.

App allows you to:

- compare your current data against ⁴_____.
- meet ⁵_____.
- try out ⁶_____.

Sleep monitor tracks ⁷_____ and ⁸_____ you sleep.

COLLABORATE

C Work with a partner. The fitness tracker upgraded the speaker's life. Complete the first row of the chart. List the new habits it helped her form and the old habits it helped her change.

Item	New habits formed	Old habits changed
Fitness tracker		

D Think of two other items that could help upgrade people's lives. Write them in the chart above. List new habits they could help people form and old habits they could help people change.

E Work with a partner. Try to convince them that the items you listed in Exercise D could help them upgrade their lives.

Checkpoint

Reflect on what you have learned. Check your progress.

I can ... understand and use words related to habits.

adjustment	adopt	consistency	discipline	fatigued
incorporate	lifestyle	modify	persevere	swap

use verb and noun forms of *adjust*, *adopt*, *modify*, and *persevere*.

watch and understand a talk about improving your life.

use visuals to guide note-taking.

listen for supporting evidence.

notice language for listing selling points.

use appropriate language to persuade a friend to break a bad habit.

collaborate and communicate effectively to persuade someone to start using a product.

An opera singer practices in front of a mirror before a performance.

Building Vocabulary

LEARN KEY WORDS

A 🎧 Listen to and read the passage below. What does the phrase *fake it till we make it* mean? What examples of this does the passage give?

We Are What We Do

Our actions don't just affect how other people see us. They affect how we see ourselves, and even shape how we feel. But can we use this to our advantage? Can we *act* a certain way—even if we don't *feel* that way—in order to change who we are? In other words, can we *fake it till we make it*? Surprisingly, the answer is yes: to some degree, we can.

Research shows that if we simply **mimic** positive behavior—for example, if we smile, stand up straight, or speak confidently—we can generate positive feelings. The opposite is also true. If we **frown** or slouch a lot, we can turn a good mood into a bad one. Our actions don't just reflect our moods: they create them. To an extent, they make us who we are.

But is this effect only temporary? It doesn't have to be. Studies indicate that doing positive things on a regular basis—in other words, making positivity a habit—can actually result in personality changes that are both **long-lasting** and **fulfilling**. And this, of course, is great for both our **emotional** and physical **well-being**.

B Work with a partner. Discuss the questions below.

1. Look at the photo and caption. How does practicing in front of a mirror help?

2. What else can you do to prepare for a big event or moment?

C Match each word in **bold** from Exercise A with its meaning.

1. _____ satisfying and rewarding

2. _____ to imitate or copy an action

3. _____ the state of one's health or happiness

4. _____ related to one's feelings

5. _____ existing for a long period of time

6. _____ to change one's facial expression to show unhappiness

D Read the excerpts from Ron Gutman's TED Talk in Lesson F. Circle the options that are closest in meaning to the words in **bold**.

1. "Smiling is one of the most basic, biologically uniform **expressions** of all humans."

   a. the moods people are feeling

   b. the looks on people's faces

2. " … subjects were asked to **determine** whether a smile was real or fake … "

   a. decide

   b. query

3. " … sent electric jolts to facial muscles to **induce** and stimulate smiles."

   a. cause something to happen

   b. change the shape of something

4. " … smiling is evolutionarily contagious, and it **suppresses** the control we usually have on our facial muscles."

   a. activates

   b. deactivates

E The words in the box collocate with the adjective **emotional**. Complete the sentences using words from the box.

state	intelligence	response	connection	support

1. He must feel horrible after the accident. I'm concerned about his emotional _____.

2. She's aware of her feelings, and those of others, too. We call that emotional _____.

3. They don't want to sell the house. They have an emotional _____ to it.

4. If you're unable to cope, your friends and family are there for emotional _____.

5. I'm embarrassed by what I said. It was an emotional _____, not a logical one.

COMMUNICATE

F Note down an example next to each prompt below. Then discuss your examples with a partner.

1. an activity you found fulfilling _____

2. something that made you frown _____

3. a time you had to suppress a laugh _____

4. how you care for your emotional well-being _____

5. a time you mimicked someone's behavior _____

G Are there limits to "fake it till you make it"? Think of a few situations in which this strategy might not work. Discuss with a partner.

> I don't think I could pretend to be a great cook and eventually succeed because …

Viewing and Note-taking

LEARNING OBJECTIVES

- Watch and understand a talk about how smiling improves our lives
- Notice how *t* and *d* sounds at the end of words are often dropped

TEDTALKS

Ron Gutman is an inventor, entrepreneur, and university professor. He has described himself as a "frequent smiler" and has explained that his mission is to help everyone live happier, healthier lives. In his TED Talk, *The Hidden Power of Smiling*, he describes many of the amazing benefits of smiling.

BEFORE VIEWING

A Work with a partner. Discuss the questions below.

1. Read the information about Ron Gutman above. What is your impression of him?

2. Gutman discusses smiling in his talk. Why do you think he calls it a "superpower"?

" Smiling stimulates our brain reward mechanism in a way that even chocolate – a well-regarded pleasure inducer – cannot match. "

WHILE VIEWING

B ▶ **LISTEN FOR MAIN IDEAS** Watch Segment 1 of Ron Gutman's TED Talk. Check (✓) the main points he makes.

1. ☐ Smiling more makes you more likely to have a successful life.

2. ☐ Smiling more helps you live a longer life.

3. ☐ People who smile are better at their jobs.

4. ☐ People everywhere smile for the same reasons.

5. ☐ Smiling often is hard to do.

6. ☐ Children smile more than adults.

C ▶ **LISTEN FOR DETAILS** Look at the notes below and try to recall the missing information. Then watch Segment 1 again and complete the notes.

SMILING IS GOOD FOR YOU

UC Berkley Study

    By studying people's smiles in old [1]_____ photos, scientists could predict:

    - how fulfilling and long-lasting their [2]_____ were.

    - how well they would score on standardized [3]_____ tests.

    - how inspiring they would be to others.

Wayne State University Research Project

    In a study of old [4]_____, the average life span of people with:

    - no smile was [5]_____ years.

    - slight smiles was [6]_____ years.

    - big smiles was [7]_____ years.

SMILING IS UNIVERSAL

    - Babies smile even before they're [8]_____.

    - People everywhere smile for the same reasons:

      - to express joy and satisfaction.

    - More than 1/3 of people smile over [9]_____ times a day.

    - Children smile about [10]_____ times a day.

WORDS IN THE TALK
aha moment (phr) when a difficult concept suddenly becomes clear
contagious (adj) spreading easily from person to person
25 grand (phr) 25,000 dollars
evolutionarily (adv) developed over thousands of generations

D ▶ **LISTEN FOR DETAILS** Read the statements below and predict if they are true or false. Then watch Segment 2 of the TED Talk and circle **T** for true or **F** for false.

1.	We mimic smiles to help us determine if a smile we're seeing is real.	**T**	**F**
2.	Charles Darwin used electric shocks to prove the benefits of smiling.	**T**	**F**
3.	Smiling stimulates our brain more than eating chocolate.	**T**	**F**
4.	Smiling reduces the amount of stress-inducing chemicals in your body.	**T**	**F**
5.	Smiling makes you look more likeable but less capable.	**T**	**F**

AFTER VIEWING

E **EVALUATE** Consider the findings in Gutman's talk. How convincing is each finding to you? Write the letters along the arrow below. Then compare your ranking with a partner, giving reasons.

a. UC Berkley yearbook findings

b. Wayne State University baseball card findings

c. how soon babies start smiling

d. the reasons people around the world smile

e. how often adults smile every day

f. how often children smile every day

not convincing   **very convincing**

PRONUNCIATION   *Dropping* t *and* d *sounds*

F 🎧 Read the sentences from the TED Talk below. Listen and circle the words with dropped *t* and *d* sounds. Then underline any other words with *t* or *d* sounds that you think could be dropped.

1. "So I used to embark on these imaginary journeys to find intergalactic objects from planet Krypton, which was a lot of fun but didn't yield much result."

2. " … as if you found 25 grand in a pocket of an old jacket you hadn't worn for ages …"

G Read the sentences. Find the words with *t* or *d* sounds at the end. Which words have *t* or *d* sounds that you think can be dropped? Discuss with a partner.

1. I didn't use to like chocolate, believe it or not.

2. She just took off without informing anyone about it.

3. They won't let us in because we don't have tickets.

4. He was late and he didn't call or text us.

> **Pronunciation Skill**
> **Dropping *t* and *d* sounds**
>
> When people speak quickly, they often drop the *t* and *d* sounds at the end of words. This is especially so when the word ends with *nt*, or when the following word begins with a consonant sound (most notably, *t* or *d*). These rules don't always apply but try to pay attention to what seems natural and comfortable.

Thinking Critically

ANALYZE INFORMATION

A Look at the infographic below. Match the smiles to the situations that best fit. Discuss with a partner.

1. _____ Duchenne
2. _____ Dampened
3. _____ Polite
4. _____ Contempt
5. _____ Fake

a. Hearing great news in a very formal situation.

b. Being in a photo after losing badly in a competition.

c. Meeting a close friend you haven't seen in a while.

d. Listening to a friend tell a boring story.

e. Meeting someone you recently had an argument with.

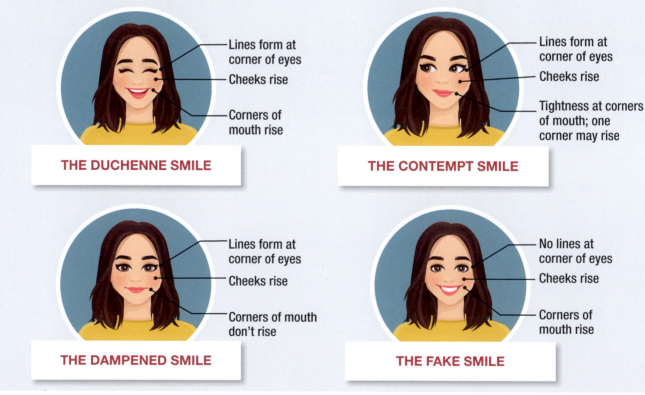

5 COMMON SMILES

THE POLITE SMILE
- No lines at corner of eyes
- Cheeks do not rise
- Corners of mouth rise slightly

THE DUCHENNE SMILE
- Lines form at corner of eyes
- Cheeks rise
- Corners of mouth rise

THE CONTEMPT SMILE
- Lines form at corner of eyes
- Cheeks rise
- Tightness at corners of mouth; one corner may rise

THE DAMPENED SMILE
- Lines form at corner of eyes
- Cheeks rise
- Corners of mouth don't rise

THE FAKE SMILE
- No lines at corner of eyes
- Cheeks rise
- Corners of mouth rise

B 🎧 Listen to a talk about types of smiles. Then circle **T** for true or **F** for false.

1. Smiling when you're not happy has no benefits.　　**T**　　**F**

2. Smiling makes a good mood better.　　**T**　　**F**

3. Fake smiling makes a bad mood worse.　　**T**　　**F**

C 🎧 Listen to an excerpt from the talk, and look at the five smiles in the infographic. Discuss with a partner.

1. Which smiles do you think are sincere?

2. Which smiles do you think are fake?

3. Which smile is hostile and not well-intentioned?

D Work with a partner. Discuss the questions below.

1. Are you able to fake a Duchenne smile? How does faking it make you feel?

2. How are you feeling today? Did fake smiling affect your mood? How?

COMMUNICATE   *Synthesize and evaluate ideas*

E Which diagram do you think best represents the ideas in the TED Talk and the ideas in this lesson? Discuss your answers and reasons with a partner.

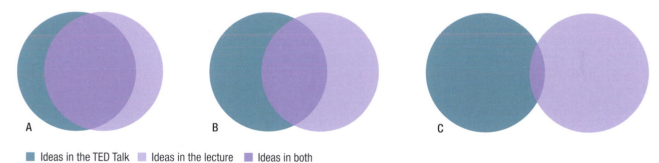

A　　　　　　　　　　B　　　　　　　　　　C

■ Ideas in the TED Talk　■ Ideas in the lecture　■ Ideas in both

F What advice would you give someone who wants to enjoy the benefits of smiling more without experiencing the downsides of fake smiling? Note down your advice. Then share your ideas with a partner.

UNIT
2
E F
G H

Putting It Together

LEARNING OBJECTIVES

• Research, plan, and present on a habit that could upgrade a person's life
• Use visuals to make presentations more interesting and fun

ASSIGNMENT

Individual presentation: You are going to give a presentation on a simple habit that has multiple benefits—physical, mental, emotional, or others.

PREPARE

A Review the unit. What are some habits and activities that can upgrade a person's life? How can these habits and activities be beneficial? Discuss with a partner.

B Research a few simple habits that can improve your life in different ways. Choose a habit that hasn't already been mentioned in the unit. Note the most interesting ideas down.

_____

_____

_____

_____

C Plan your presentation. Choose your best idea from Exercise B. Then complete the chart below.

Habit	
Mental benefits	
Emotional benefits	
Physical benefits	
Other benefits	

D Look back at the vocabulary, pronunciation, and communication skills you've learned in this unit. What can you use in your presentation? Note any useful language below.

_____

_____

_____

_____

_____

E Below are some ideas of visuals that could help liven up a presentation. Think about which ones are suitable for your presentation and add them to your plan.

| photos | videos | charts | infographics |
| gifs | memes | icons | illustrations |

F Practice your presentation. Make use of the presentation skill that you've learned.

PRESENT

G Give your presentation to a partner. Watch their presentation and evaluate them using the Presentation Scoring Rubrics at the back of the book.

H Discuss your evaluation with your partner. Give feedback on two things they did well and two areas for improvement.

Checkpoint

Reflect on what you have learned. Check your progress.

I can ... ☐ understand and use words related to feelings and behavior.

| **determine** | **emotional** | **expression** | **frown** | **fulfilling** |
| **induce** | **long-lasting** | **mimic** | **suppress** | **well-being** |

☐ use collocations with the word _emotional_.

☐ watch and understand a talk about how smiling improves our lives.

☐ notice how _t_ and _d_ sounds at the end of words are often dropped.

☐ interpret an infographic about different types of smiles.

☐ synthesize and evaluate ideas about the effects of smiling.

☐ use visuals to make presentations more interesting and fun.

☐ give a presentation on a habit that could upgrade a person's life.

Young people have an animated discussion in sign language in Serbia.

3

More than Words

Q How can we communicate better?

Complex and rich communication is one of the key things that makes us human. We have many communicative tools at our disposal: we can communicate in speaking, writing, or even in sign language, like the people in the photo. And sometimes we don't need to use words at all: body language, facial expressions and gestures can convey volumes. Every day we have dozens of interactions where we rely on our communication skills to get our message across. But are we always successful? In this unit, we look at why communication sometimes goes wrong and what we can do to communicate–and listen–more effectively.

THINK and DISCUSS

1 Look at the photo and read the caption. How are the people in the photo communicating? Do you know how to communicate this way?

2 Look at the essential question and the unit introduction. Do you think you are an effective communicator? What do you think are your strengths and weaknesses?

Building Vocabulary

LEARNING OBJECTIVES

• Use ten words related to communication
• Understand the different meanings of *objective* and *grasp*

LEARN KEY WORDS

A 🎧 Listen to and read the information below. Discuss the questions with a partner.

1. Which mistake in the passage do you think was the most careless? Why?
2. Which "Cs of communication" did the organizations not adhere to?
3. Has a miscommunication ever caused problems for you? What happened?

Costly Communication Disasters

Human **interaction** is complex, and it's **subjective**, too: people often have different **interpretations** of the same message. As a result, poor communication often leads to **confusion**—and sometimes, much worse.

A $125 Million Space Disaster

In 1999, NASA launched a probe into space to study the planet Mars. The probe was designed to orbit the planet 150 kilometers above its surface. However, when it finally arrived at Mars, things went wrong. The probe flew too close to the planet and eventually burned up in its atmosphere. What caused the miscalculation? A simple failure to agree on units of measurement. One team of engineers used the imperial unit *pounds*, while everyone else used the metric unit *Newtons*.

Million Dollar Discounts

The flight from Toronto to Cyprus is long and expensive. So imagine everyone's surprise when tickets that should have cost $3,900 went for $39 instead! The airline realized its error quickly and even **acknowledged** it publicly, but not before losing $7 million. A similar mistake happened in Japan when a company offered to sell 610,000 of its shares for one yen each. It had meant to sell each of its shares for 610,000 yen! In less than a day, the company lost $340 million.

Six Cs of Effective Communication

Communication should be ...

1 CLEAR
• Use simple language when possible.
• Avoid vague or subjective phrasing.

2 COMPLETE
• Give all the information listeners need.
• Provide context when necessary.

3 CONCISE
• Avoid long-winded sentences.
• Leave out unnecessary details.

4 CONSIDERATE
• Think about the listener's feelings.
• Pay attention to the tone of your message.

5 CORRECT
• Check that your information is accurate.
• Be honest if you're not sure.

6 CONSTRUCTIVE
• Try not to cause or prolong arguments.
• Try to create positive outcomes.

B Complete the definitions below using the correct form of each word in **bold** from Exercise A.

1. When you _____ something, you indicate that you are aware of it.

2. A(n) _____ refers to an exchange between two or more people.

3. A person's _____ is what they think something is or means.

4. If something is _____, it is influenced by personal opinion.

5. _____ occurs when messages or instructions are unclear.

C Read the passage. Then match the words in **bold** to their meanings.

Our **perception** of things is influenced by subjective factors, so in general, try to be more **objective** when communicating. Don't assume the other person knows what you know or feels the same way you do. Help others **grasp** what you're trying to say by bridging the gaps between you and them. Consider their backgrounds, and **facilitate** communication by taking into account individual perspectives and paying attention to verbal and non-verbal **feedback**.

1. _____ perception
2. _____ objective
3. _____ grasp
4. _____ facilitate
5. _____ feedback

a. information given in response to something
b. to help make something happen smoothly
c. not influenced by personal feelings
d. to understand something
e. how people see or understand something

D The words **objective** and **grasp** each have more than one meaning. Read the sentences below. Do the words in **bold** have the same meanings as in Exercise C? Circle **S** (same) or **D** (different).

1. This essay is confusing. You need to make your **objective** clear.   S   D

2. This essay is quite biased. You need to be more **objective**.   S   D

3. He failed to **grasp** what the rope on the tree was for.   S   D

4. He failed to **grasp** the rope that was hanging from the tree.   S   D

COMMUNICATE

E Work in a group. Discuss the questions.

1. Look at the Six Cs of Effective Communication again. Which do you find easiest? Which is most difficult? Why?

2. When is each "C" particularly important? Think of six situations.

For me, being considerate is the easiest. I'm always polite.

I think being constructive is most important when you disagree with someone.

Viewing and Note-taking

LEARNING OBJECTIVES

- Watch a talk about miscommunication
- Focus on essential ideas and details when taking notes
- Understand analogies

BEFORE VIEWING

A  Listen to a person talking about communication. Make notes as you listen. Keep your notes brief. Include only main ideas and essential details.

The survey is about:

_____

_____

Finding 1: _____

_____

_____

Finding 2: _____

_____

_____

Finding 3: _____

_____

_____

> **Note-taking Skill**
> **Focusing on Essential Ideas and Details**
>
> Include main ideas and essential details in your notes, and leave out unnecessary information. For instance, some analogies are long, but we don't need to note down every detail. Often, a brief description is sufficient.

Communication is similar to a game of catch.

WHILE VIEWING

B ▶ **LISTEN FOR MAIN IDEAS** Watch the TED-Ed video and complete the notes below.

How does communication work?

Model 1: ¹_____

Like a person ²_____ to someone and walking away.

– Does not reflect the ³_____ of human interaction.

Model 2: ⁴_____

Like a game of ⁵_____ played with a lump of ⁶_____.

– We ⁷_____ the message as it goes back and forth.

Four tips:

1. Engage ⁸_____ while you listen.

2. Listen with your ⁹_____, ears, and gut.

3. Take time to ¹⁰_____ before speaking.

4. Be aware of your perceptual filters.

C UNDERSTAND ANALOGIES Look at your notes above.

1. What analogy is used to explain the transmission model?
2. What analogy is used to explain the transactional model?
3. Do the analogies work well? Can you think of other analogies that describe communication?

D ▶ **LISTEN FOR DETAILS** Read the four tips in Exercise B. Then watch an excerpt from the TED-Ed video. Match the tips to the explanations below.

Tip 1: _____   **a.** Don't rush to speak. Be open to what others say.

Tip 2: _____   **b.** Pay attention to more than just words.

Tip 3: _____   **c.** Express your view, but ask how others see it, too.

Tip 4: _____   **d.** Pay attention to feedback. Adjust your message.

AFTER VIEWING

E APPLY Work with a partner. Read the situations. Which tip from Exercise D do you think is most useful in each situation?

1. You're a patient. You're listening to a doctor explain a complicated health condition.
2. You're talking to someone who is quite upset with a close friend.
3. You're planning a vacation with friends. One friend was robbed the last time he traveled.
4. The company president visits your office and asks you what you'd like to see improved.

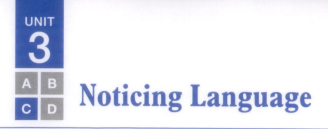

Noticing Language

LISTEN FOR LANGUAGE *Use contrast*

A 🎧 Listen to an excerpt from the TED-Ed Talk in Lesson B. Discuss with a partner.

> **Communication Skill**
> **Using Contrast**
>
> Contrast can help us define some things by illustrating what these things are not. Contrast can be used to describe something as basic as a simple opinion, or it can help make a complex idea easier to understand.

1. The speaker covers the transmission model rather briefly before dismissing it. Why bring it up at all?

2. How would the explanation have been different if the speaker had not mentioned the transmission model?

B Read the expressions in the box below. Answer the questions.

1. What common three-letter word could we also use to express contrast?

2. Which four expressions are good for contrasting a simplistic idea with a more accurate one?

Actually, …	However, …
In contrast, …	In reality, …
On the other hand, …	Conversely, …
It's more accurate to (say that) …	A better way to look at it would be …

C 🎧 Listen to two talks. Complete the sentences with the words you hear. Then work with a partner. Which other words and expressions from Exercise B can you use?

Talk 1

1. Languages like English have different verb forms to indicate tense. For example, the word *take* has three forms: *take*, *took*, and *taken*. _____, many other languages don't have past tense verbs.

2. So in English, you might say something like "I went to the market yesterday." _____, in languages like Indonesian or Mandarin, you'd probably say something like "I go to the market yesterday."

Talk 2

3. It's common to hear people compare the human brain to a computer. In this analogy, our thoughts are like files that we arrange in neat folders. _____ to think of your brain as the internet.

4. The first analogy is too simple to describe complex human thinking. _____, the second analogy better accounts for why human behavior is so unpredictable.

COMMUNICATE

D Work with a partner. Read the sentences. Think of possible ways to complete them.

1. Many people feel that it is rude to interrupt others. However, …

_____

2. My brother often communicates in an aggressive way. In contrast, my sister …

_____

3. If you work alone, you'll probably finish your work quicker. On the other hand, …

_____

4. Many people think that hard work guarantees success. In reality, …

_____

E Work with a partner. Read the situations and the two opposing strategies for each situation. Which strategy do you think is better? Use contrast to help explain your opinion.

1. You're in a meeting. You want to find out why something went wrong so you can fix it.

   a. Speak directly and honestly.　　　**b.** Speak carefully to avoid upsetting others.

2. You need to give a short thank you speech to your colleagues.

   a. Write and read it out word for word.　　**b.** Prepare a loose outline and speak naturally.

3. You need to explain something complicated to someone.

   a. Send one long email.　　　　　**b.** Send several short emails.

Communicating Ideas

ASSIGNMENT

Task: You are going to collaborate with a partner to understand and fix a communication problem between two people.

LISTEN FOR INFORMATION

A Work with a partner. Read the emails. Then answer the questions.

1. Overall, how do you think the meeting went?
2. What do you think Mateus did well?
3. What do you think Mateus could have done better?

From: Oksana B.

To: Mateus R.

Subject: Yesterday's Meeting

Hi Mateus,

How was the meeting with Mr. Leong?

Oksana

From: Mateus R.

To: Oksana B.

Subject: Re: Yesterday's Meeting

Hi Oksana,

Mr. Leong doesn't really talk much so it's hard to be absolutely sure, but I think it went well. We stayed longer than planned, which was promising. I was able to explain in great detail all the ways we could help boost his sales. I even spent time on less conventional ideas that we hadn't discussed previously, to show we were considering every possible solution. I gave Mr. Leong all the reassurance and information he needed, so I'm hopeful we made a good impression. I'm expecting a call from him soon.

Mateus

B Read Mateus's email again. Is it possible that he was wrong about how the meeting went? Discuss with a partner.

C 🎧 Listen to a conversation between Mr. Leong and his colleague Raul. Then work with a partner. Compare how Mateus and Mr. Leong felt about the meeting.

	Mateus	Mr. Leong
Duration:	_____	_____
Topics discussed:	_____	_____
Feelings about meeting:	_____	_____

D Work with a partner. Look at your answers in Exercise A. Which, if any, would you change?

E What could Mr. Leong have done differently to make the meeting go better? Discuss with a partner. Then contrast Mr. Leong's mistakes and Mateus's.

COLLABORATE

F After speaking with Raul, Mr. Leong decides to meet Mateus again. What should Mr. Leong and Mateus do for their second meeting to go better? Discuss with a partner.

Mr. Leong

Mateus

Checkpoint

Reflect on what you have learned. Check your progress.

I can ... ☐ understand and use words related to communication.

acknowledge	confusion	facilitate	feedback	grasp
interaction	interpretation	objective	perception	subjective

☐ use the different meanings of *objective* and *grasp*.

☐ watch and understand a talk about miscommunication.

☐ focus on essential ideas and details when taking notes.

☐ understand analogies while listening.

☐ notice the use of contrast to define a concept.

☐ use contrast to explain how I would handle different situations.

☐ collaborate and communicate effectively to help solve a communication problem.

A counselor listens to a woman describe her family problems on a "Friendship Bench" in Zimbabwe.

Building Vocabulary

LEARN KEY WORDS

A  Listen to and read the passage below. What are two reasons why charities sometimes don't help? According to the writer, how can charities operate better?

A Band-Aid Solution?

Millions suffer around the world because they lack the **resources** to escape the effects of poverty, disease, and war. Thankfully, there are many people who care. Governments and charities help provide **aid**, while **donors** and volunteers do what they can to make a difference.

To most of us, charity is crucial if we are to make the world a better place. But many experts and government officials feel differently. To them, charity is more of a band-aid solution: it addresses the issues we see without fixing the underlying problems. And while some people may still benefit from charity, it does not necessarily lead to long-term improvement. Charity can even slow progress down because local organizations and officials who benefit from foreign aid have little incentive to **initiate** sustainable, locally-driven change.

So how can charities do their jobs better? The debate is ongoing, but a few things are clear: **passion** and good intentions are often not enough. **Cooperation** with local communities is key.

B Work with a partner. Discuss the questions below.

1. What are some charities you know?
2. Have you heard any negative stories about charities?
3. Look at the photo. It shows a person receiving free counseling from a trained local volunteer. How does a charity like this help people? Do you think it contributes to the types of problems described in the passage?

C Match the correct form of each word in **bold** from Exercise A with its meaning.

1. _____ something given to help others, like food or money

2. _____ to begin something

3. _____ someone who gives money in support of a cause

4. _____ money, equipment, or materials needed to do something

5. _____ working closely together in a coordinated way

6. _____ a strong and powerful feeling about something

D Read the passage below. Then circle the meanings of the words in **bold**.

How can charities better help people in need? Here are some simple principles. First, don't be **patronizing**. You don't know better just because you're richer or more fortunate. Second, treat the people you're helping as **clients**, not employees. Don't tell them what to do. Find out what new **enterprises** *they* would like to set up. And third, get to know the people you're serving. Have **one-on-one** conversations with them, and find out what their hopes and concerns are.

1. If you're being **patronizing**, you're talking to someone as if you're …

    a. better than them   **b.** paying for them

2. If you're with a **client**, you're with someone who …

    a. works for you   **b.** you work for

3. If you create an **enterprise**, you ….

    a. start a business   **b.** build a structure

4. If you're in a **one-on-one** conversation, you're ….

    a. trying to speak very quickly   **b.** talking to an individual

E The prefix *co-* indicates that something is done together. Complete the sentences below with the *co-* words from the box.

co-author	co-own	coexist	cooperate

1. They're equal partners who _____ the restaurant.

2. We can't do this alone. We need to _____.

3. Lara wrote the book with the help of a _____.

4. The two nations need to find a way to _____ peacefully.

COMMUNICATE

F Note an example next to each prompt below. Discuss with a partner and ask follow-up questions.

    1. something you have a passion for   _____

    2. something you do that requires cooperation   _____

    3. an enterprise you think could succeed   _____

    4. a time someone was patronizing toward you   _____

G Work with a partner. Think of a need in your community and an idea for a charity to help address this need. Would your idea contribute to the problems raised in Exercise A?

> Many young people can't afford college. We could get donors to help buy them the books they need.

> But that's an expensive solution. How about …

Viewing and Note-taking

LEARNING OBJECTIVES

- Watch and understand a talk about the power of effective listening
- Use pauses for effect

TEDTALKS

Ernesto Sirolli is an expert on sustainable economic development. In 1985, he pioneered an economic development model that taps into the passion and resourcefulness of locals. Since then, his model has helped over 250 communities worldwide. In his TED Talk, *Want to Help Someone? Shut Up and Listen!*, he explains the importance of listening when helping others.

BEFORE VIEWING

A Read the information about Ernesto Sirolli and look at the quotation in the picture. Discuss the questions below with a partner.

1. Why do you think it is difficult to "shut up and listen"?
2. Are most people good listeners? Why, or why not?
3. Why is listening important when trying to help others?

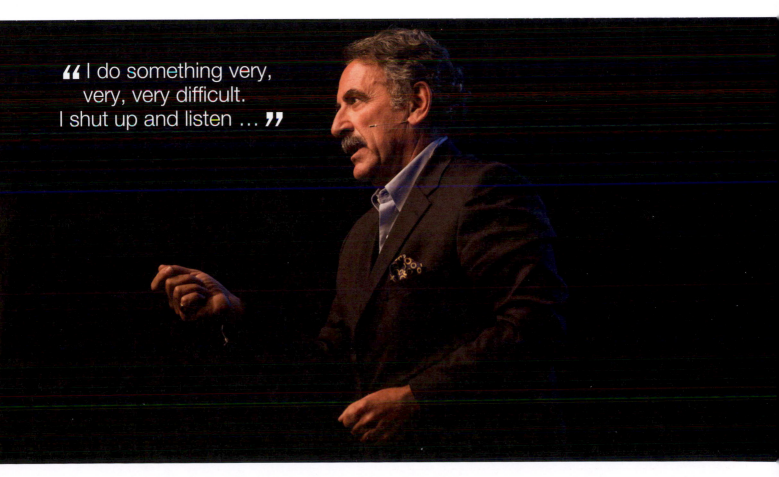

" I do something very, very, very difficult. I shut up and listen ... "

WHILE VIEWING

B ▶ **LISTEN FOR MAIN IDEAS** Watch Segment 1 of Ernesto Sirolli's TED Talk. Why does Sirolli share this story? Check (✓) the likely reasons.

1. ☐ to explain that helping is pointless unless we do it correctly
2. ☐ to describe the important work charities around the world do
3. ☐ to explain that location is very important when growing crops
4. ☐ to explain that locals understand the challenges they face

C ▶ **SEQUENCE EVENTS** Read the sentences below. Then watch Segment 1 again. Order the events below (1–7).

a. _____ Sirolli taught the locals how to farm the land.

b. _____ The locals said nobody consulted them.

c. _____ Sirolli found that the area near the Zambezi river was fertile.

d. _____ Hippos ate all the tomatoes by the river.

e. _____ Sirolli learned that many others were helping people the wrong way.

f. _____ Sirolli was surprised nobody had warned them.

g. _____ The seeds that were planted there grew very well.

D ▶ Watch Segment 2 of Sirolli's TED Talk. Then read the statements about Enterprise Facilitation. What does Sirolli say we should do? Check (✓) the correct answers.

1. ☐ Set up an office as a base of operations.
2. ☐ Hold community meetings.
3. ☐ Meet locals one-on-one.
4. ☐ Meet in informal locations.
5. ☐ Suggest new business ideas.
6. ☐ Connect locals to knowledge and resources.

E ▶ Watch Segment 3 of Sirolli's TED Talk. Listen to how Sirolli helped one community in Esperance, Australia. Then complete the flowchart, using your own words where necessary.

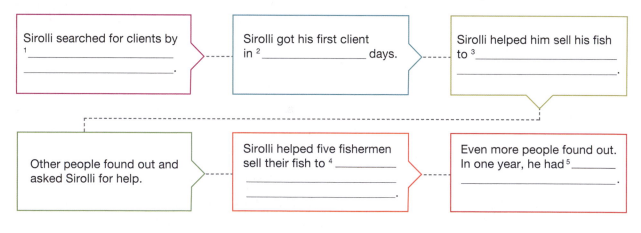

Sirolli searched for clients by ¹_____ _____.

Sirolli got his first client in ²_____ days.

Sirolli helped him sell his fish to ³_____ _____.

Other people found out and asked Sirolli for help.

Sirolli helped five fishermen sell their fish to ⁴_____ _____ _____.

Even more people found out. In one year, he had ⁵_____ _____.

WORDS IN THE TALK

NGO (n) non-governmental organization; often a charity
distraught (adj) very upset
infrastructure (n) the physical parts of an organization
entrepreneur (n) someone who starts their own business

AFTER VIEWING

F Put yourself in Sirolli's shoes. Imagine a farmer came to you expressing a desire to grow his business. What would you do? What wouldn't you do? Discuss with a partner, and complete the chart below.

DO	DON'T

> So if a farmer came to you wanting to grow his business, what would you do?

> First I would definitely ask him to talk about want he wants to do …

PRONUNCIATION *Use pauses for effect*

G 🎧 Look at the quotations from Sirolli's talk. Guess where the long pauses are. Then listen to confirm. Add two slashes (//) where you hear long pauses.

1. "I worked for an Italian NGO, and every single project that we set up in Africa failed."

2. "I thought, age 21, that we Italians were good people, and we were doing good work in Africa. Instead, everything we touched we killed."

3. "Our first project, the one that has inspired my first book, *Ripples from the Zambezi*, was a project where we Italians decided to teach Zambian people how to grow food."

Pronunciation Skill
Pausing for Effect

Pausing for effect gives listeners time to absorb and consider a point. Speakers use long pauses to introduce new ideas, highlight key information, emphasize the punchline of a joke, or heighten interest in what they're about to say.

H Read the sentences below. Add two slashes (//) where you think a long pause would be good. Then work with a partner. Read the sentences out loud to each other. Did you pause in the same places?

1. My secret to being a good communicator? It's really simple, actually. Always listen more than you speak.

2. Do they really need our help? Of course they do. But what kind of help do they need? It's important that the kind of help we give isn't patronizing.

3. There are three rules I follow as a business owner. Rule 1: The customer is always right. Rule 2: Always serve with a smile. And Rule 3: When in doubt, refer to Rule 1.

Thinking Critically

ANALYZE INFORMATION

A Look at the infographic below and answer the questions. Think of reasons for your answers. Then discuss with a partner.

1. Which listening style best describes how *you* listen?

2. Is it possible to have more than one listening style?

3. Can people with different listening styles work well with each other?

What is your listening style?

Action-focused listeners are more interested in what needs to be done than they are in the reasons or supporting evidence. They dislike messages that are long-winded or disorganized.

Content-focused listeners are interested in logic and accuracy. They break down complex messages and seek other perspectives before making decisions. They prefer listening to people they know to be thorough.

People-focused listeners focus on the emotions and concerns of the speaker. They want to find common ground and strengthen relationships. They are not critical or judgmental, and are easy to trust and confide in.

Time-focused listeners want messages that get to the point quickly. They are efficient and focused on deadlines. They make decisions quickly as soon as they feel they have all the info they need.

B 🎧 Listen to a talk about listening styles. Then work with a partner. The speaker describes two situations. Which listening style do you think is best suited for each situation? Rank them from 1 (most suited) to 4 (least suited).

Situation 1: ___ Action-focused   ___ Content-focused   ___ People-focused   ___ Time-focused

Situation 2: ___ Action-focused   ___ Content-focused   ___ People-focused   ___ Time-focused

C Work in a group. The speaker claims that each listening style has strengths and blind spots. What do you think some of these are? Do you need to work on any of these blind spots?

ACTION-FOCUSED	CONTENT-FOCUSED
Strengths:	Strengths:
Blind spots:	Blind spots:
PEOPLE-FOCUSED	**TIME-FOCUSED**
Strengths:	Strengths:
Blind spots:	Blind spots:

COMMUNICATE *Synthesize and evaluate ideas*

D Work in a group. Think about Ernesto Sirolli's TED Talk. Discuss the questions.

1. Imagine applying each listening style to the work Sirolli describes. How would the outcomes differ?
2. Which two listening styles do you think are best suited for the type of work Sirolli describes?

E Work with a partner. Look at your chart in Exercise C. Then think of situations for which each listening style is well-suited and poorly suited.

	Well suited	Poorly suited
1. Action-focused	_____	_____
2. Content-focused	_____	_____
3. People-focused	_____	_____
4. Time-focused	_____	_____

A people-focused listener would be great when I'm sad and need someone to talk to.

Right, but when there is a crisis, I want an action-focused listener.

UNIT
3

E F
G H

Putting It Together

LEARNING OBJECTIVES

- Research, plan, and present on how listening more would benefit particular groups of people
- Use gestures to make presentations more engaging

ASSIGNMENT

Group presentation: Your group is going to give a presentation on how one group of people might benefit if another group were to "shut up and listen" to them more.

PREPARE

A Review the unit. What do you think are the three most important communication tips mentioned? Discuss with a partner.

1. _____ **2.** _____ **3.** _____

B Work with your group. Look at the groups of people below. How would the people on the left benefit if the people on the right tried harder to "shut up and listen"? Note down one way for each pairing. You can also come up with your own groups and note down ideas for them.

1. students / teachers _____

2. children / parents _____

3. patients / doctors _____

4. customers / companies _____

5. _____ / _____ _____

6. _____ / _____ _____

C Plan your presentation. Choose two of your best ideas from Exercise B and complete the charts.

IDEA 1: _____ might benefit if _____ shut up and listened to them. Here's how …		
Problem	**What causes it**	**How listening more would help**

IDEA 2: _____ might benefit if _____ shut up and listened to them. Here's how …		
Problem	**What causes it**	**How listening more would help**

D Look back at the vocabulary, pronunciation, and communication skills you've learned in this unit. What can you use in your presentation? Note any useful language below.

_____

_____

_____

E Below are some examples of gestures. Think about which of these you could use in your presentation.

DESCRIPTIVE Spreading your hands apart to show length or time, or pointing up to show an increase.	**EMOTIONAL** Holding your hand to your heart to show passion, or raising your arms to show joy.
SYMBOLIC Holding up your hand to signify stopping, or using your fingers to show numbers.	**ILLUSTRATIVE** Pretending to eat something, or typing in the air to illustrate sending an email.

Presentation Skill
Using Gestures Effectively
Gestures are movements you make with your hands. In Ernesto Sirolli's TED Talk, he often uses gestures to add meaning, emotion, passion, and emphasis to his words. Gestures help make presentations more engaging.

F Practice your presentation. Make use of the presentation skill that you've learned.

PRESENT

G Give your presentation to another group. Watch their presentation and evaluate them using the Presentation Scoring Rubrics at the back of the book.

H Discuss your evaluation with the other group. Give feedback on two things they did well and two areas for improvement.

Checkpoint

Reflect on what you have learned. Check your progress.

I can ... understand and use words related to charity.

aid	client	cooperation	donor	enterprise
initiate	one-on-one	passion	patronizing	resources

use verbs and nouns with the prefix *co-*.

watch and understand a talk about the power of effective listening.

use pauses for effect.

interpret an infographic about different listening styles.

synthesize and evaluate ideas about listening effectively.

use gestures to make presentations more engaging.

give a presentation on how listening more would benefit particular groups of people.

A worker adds a new coat of paint to the Golden Gate Bridge in San Francisco, U.S.A.

4

Risk Takers

Q When are risks worth taking?

The worker in this photo has a risky job. He clearly faces real danger as he carries out his work high up on the Golden Gate Bridge in San Francisco, U.S.A. However, not all risks are so obvious. In fact, it is easy to overlook many of the risks we take every day, from just crossing the street to eating too much junk food. Risk is everywhere, so it's important that we're able to assess it logically. In this unit, we look at the science of risk-taking and explore ways we can make better decisions when weighing risks.

THINK and DISCUSS

1 Look at the photo and read the caption. What is the person doing, and what are some of the risks involved?

2 Look at the essential question and the unit introduction. What are some of the everyday risks that *you* take?

Building Vocabulary

LEARN KEY WORDS

A 🎧 Listen to and read the information below. Discuss with a partner.

1. What were your initial responses? Which options did you choose and why?
2. Did you change your mind when you thought about the situations more objectively? Why?
3. Are the risks involved in situations 1 and 2 any different?

WHAT WOULD YOU DO?

Imagine you're a participant in a game show. You've already won a thousand dollars when you're offered a bonus prize. You're presented with two options:

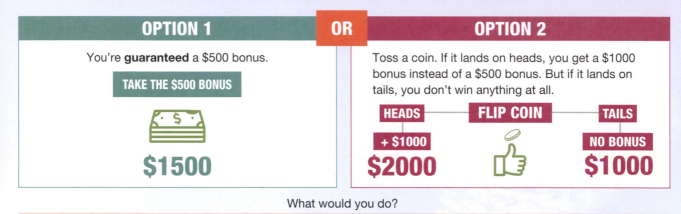

OPTION 1	OR	OPTION 2
You're **guaranteed** a $500 bonus.		Toss a coin. If it lands on heads, you get a $1000 bonus instead of a $500 bonus. But if it lands on tails, you don't win anything at all.
TAKE THE $500 BONUS		**HEADS** — **FLIP COIN** — **TAILS**
		+ $1000 👍 **NO BONUS**
$1500		**$2000** **$1000**

What would you do?

It's now later in the game, and you've managed to accrue $2000! Unfortunately, you've incurred a penalty. You have two options:

OPTION 1	OR	OPTION 2
You're guaranteed a $500 loss.		Toss a coin. If it lands on heads, you lose nothing. But if it lands on tails, you incur a $1000 loss instead of a $500 loss.
TAKE THE $500 LOSS		**HEADS** — **FLIP COIN** — **TAILS**
		LOSE NOTHING 👍 **- $1000**
$1500		**$2000** **$1000**

What would you do?

In situations like these, our **intuition** often kicks in and we make decisions based on gut feelings. But such decisions aren't always **rational**. We're not thinking objectively about the risks involved and the **probability** of each **outcome**—we're making snap decisions based on emotions and past experiences.

So, think about the game show scenarios again, but this time, without any emotion or **bias**. What would you do this time?

B Match each word in **bold** from Exercise A with its meaning.

1. _____ definitely going to happen

2. _____ the likelihood of an outcome

3. _____ based on logic

4. _____ the result of something

5. _____ an often unfair preference for or prejudice against something

6. _____ a strong, inner feeling that tells you what to do or what is true

C Read the words in **bold** and their definitions. Then complete the passage using the correct words.

aversion: a dislike or fear of something	**mental:** relating to the mind
odds: the likelihood of something happening	**phenomenon:** an event that is noteworthy

Assessing risk can be a tricky [1]_____ exercise. In the game show scenario earlier, the two coin tosses *feel* different, but when you think about it, what was at stake was exactly the same. You stand to either gain or lose $500 by tossing the coin. The [2]_____ are the same, too: you have a 50-50 chance of guessing correctly each time. Yet, for many people, a(n) [3]_____ to losing affects their judgment. The guaranteed $500 loss seems so much more significant than the guaranteed $500 bonus that more people are willing to toss a coin to avoid the loss. There's a name that describes this [4]_____: it's called loss aversion.

D There are many idioms that use the word **odds**. Read the sentences on the left. Then match them with the idioms on the right.

1. _____ I'm sure you'll make it.
2. _____ There's too much to do in too little time.
3. _____ I don't know how you did it.
4. _____ Oh, wow. It's you again.

a. You succeeded against the odds.
b. What are the odds?
c. The odds are in your favor.
d. The odds are stacked against you.

COMMUNICATE

E Note an example next to each prompt below. Discuss with a partner.

1. a situation with an unexpected outcome _____
2. a decision you made that wasn't rational _____
3. a time you succeeded against the odds _____
4. something in life that is guaranteed to happen _____

F Work in a group. Think of a time you didn't listen to your intuition when perhaps you should have. Describe what happened and what you would do differently if faced with the decision again.

Viewing and Note-taking

LEARNING OBJECTIVES

• Watch a video about irrational decisions
• Write notes about technical terms
• Understand technical terms

BEFORE VIEWING

A 🎧 Listen to a talk that contains several technical terms that the speaker explains. Write down their meanings.

1. cognition _____

2. cognitive bias _____

3. subconscious _____

4. confirmation bias _____

> **Listening Skill**
> **Understanding Technical Terms**
>
> When you hear an unfamiliar technical term, don't panic. Speakers generally explain the technical terms they use. And even if they don't, you can always use context to help you understand—the same way you would for any new word.

WHILE VIEWING

B ▶ **LISTEN FOR MAIN IDEAS** Watch the TED-Ed video. Which statement below best summarizes the video?

a. Loss aversion can cause us to apply heuristics in ways that aren't always rational.

b. Heuristics can be useful, but they can also cause us to make complex decisions poorly.

c. Heuristics can help us to make decisions based on logic instead of intuition.

C ▶ **LISTEN FOR TECHNICAL TERMS** Watch the TED-Ed video again. Listen for the technical terms below and make notes on their meanings. Then check with a partner and discuss the following:

• What abbreviations could you use for them?

• What examples were used?

> **Note-taking Skill**
> **Noting Technical Terms**
>
> When noting down technical terms, there are a few strategies that can help. For instance, pay attention to visuals to help with their spelling, and note down definitions and brief examples that help explain them. Use simple abbreviations for the technical terms in later notes, to save time. At home, research the term more fully and use what you learn to review and improve your notes.

Loss aversion: _____

_____

Heuristics: _____

_____

Conjunction fallacy: _____

_____

Anchoring effect: _____

_____

D Use your notes from Exercise C to complete the mind map below. Write the missing technical terms.

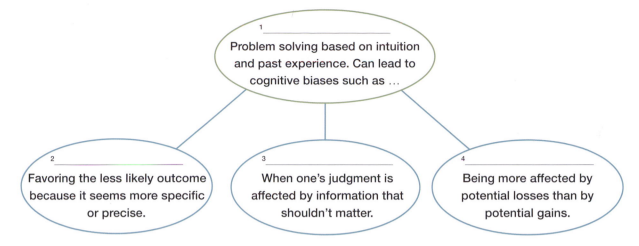

1 _____

Problem solving based on intuition and past experience. Can lead to cognitive biases such as …

2 _____

Favoring the less likely outcome because it seems more specific or precise.

3 _____

When one's judgment is affected by information that shouldn't matter.

4 _____

Being more affected by potential losses than by potential gains.

E ▶ **LISTEN FOR DETAILS** Watch the TED-Ed video again. Choose the correct option to complete the sentences.

1. In the game show scenario, most people prefer to accept the guaranteed **bonus / loss**.

2. In the experiment with the red and green dice, more people chose the **shorter / longer** sequence.

3. The **conjunction fallacy / anchoring effect** is often used to raise prices.

4. Heuristics help us to **make decisions quickly / analyze situations logically**.

5. When faced with complex problems, we should **shut off / be aware of** our brains' heuristics.

AFTER VIEWING

F **APPLY** Work with a partner. Look at the two quotations below. Which cognitive biases are they examples of? Can you think of other real-world examples of these biases?

"I don't like the idea of investing my money for higher gains. I'm aware there are low-risk investment options out there, but I'd rather just keep my money in the bank where I know it's definitely safe."

"I need an extra week for a job done, but if I ask for a week, my boss will only give me two or three days. So I'll say I need two weeks. That way, I'm more likely to get the one week I need."

Noticing Language

LISTEN FOR LANGUAGE   *Help listeners follow ideas*

A 🎧 Listen to three excerpts from the TED-Ed video in Lesson B. Match each excerpt (1–3) to what the excerpt does (a–c).

Excerpt 1: _____   Excerpt 2: _____   Excerpt 3: _____

a. gives a useful example

b. defines a key concept

c. asks and answers a question listeners might have

> ### Communication Skill
> **Helping Listeners Follow Ideas**
>
> As a speaker, you should always try to make it as easy as possible for listeners to understand you. You can do this by defining key terms and concepts, giving useful examples, or asking and answering questions listeners might have.

B Look at the expressions in the box. What is the function of each expression? Add them to the chart below.

refer(s) to ...	For example, ...	But how ... ?
For instance, ...	We call this ...	So, is there ... ?
This is what's called ...	This is an example of ...	

Defining or naming terms or concepts	
Giving examples to support ideas	
Asking questions listeners might have	

C 🎧 Listen to a talk and complete the sentences with the expressions you hear. Then work with a partner. Can you use other expressions from Exercise B to complete the sentences?

1. The word *fallacy* is used to _____ reasoning that's flawed. And there are many logical fallacies we need to be aware of.

2. _____, people often incorrectly assume that some actions have inevitable and irreversible negative consequences. _____ the slippery slope fallacy.

3. Also, many people assume that if one thing happens after another thing, then the first thing must have caused the second thing to happen. _____ the causal fallacy.

4. _____ anything we can do to avoid logical fallacies? As it turns out, there are quite a few things you can do. _____, try disagreeing with yourself.

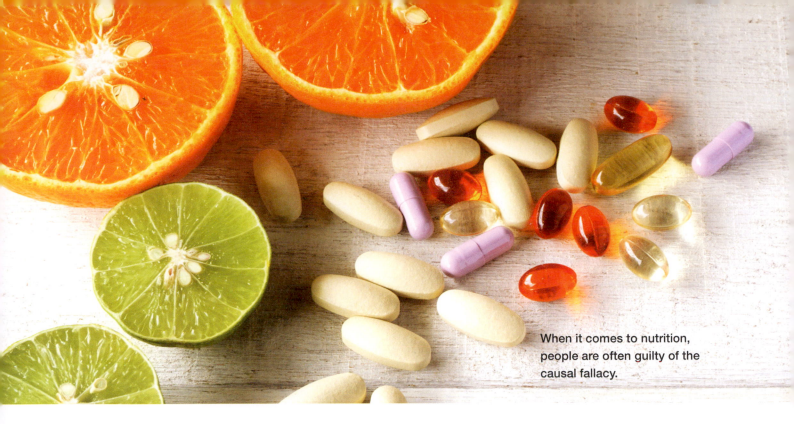

When it comes to nutrition, people are often guilty of the causal fallacy.

COMMUNICATE

D Work with a partner. Read the sentences below. Complete them using your own ideas.

1. Everybody takes risks every day. For instance, _____.

2. It's best then not to rely on intuition when weighing risks. So, _____?

3. _____ refers to _____.

4. _____. This is an example of an educated risk.

E Work individually. Choose one of the topics below to explain to a partner. Make notes on definitions you need to give, examples you could use, and questions your partner might have that you could ask and answer.

extreme sports	risky jobs	dangerous places	dangerous pets

_____

_____

_____

_____

_____

F Work with a partner who chose a different topic in Exercise E. Take turns to give a short talk about each of your topics. Use your notes and the language from Exercise B to help you.

> "Extreme sports" refers to sports with a high amount of risk …

Communicating Ideas

ASSIGNMENT

Task: You are going to collaborate in a group to identify and explain some risks that are often misunderstood as more or less dangerous than they really are.

LISTEN FOR INFORMATION

A 🎧 **LISTEN FOR MAIN IDEAS** Listen to a talk. What is the main idea of the talk? Circle the answer.

    a. Fear clouds our judgment, so we should assess risk using data.

    b. The risk of flying is much less than the risk of driving.

    c. The world is much less dangerous than we think it is.

B 🎧 **LISTEN FOR DETAILS** Listen again and complete the notes below.

> Flying seems risky because plane crashes are horrible.
>
> But stats paint a different picture:
>
> - Flying is the _____.
>
> - Much safer than _____.
>
> We attach more risk to scarier things:
>
> _____
>
> _____

C Do you know anyone who's afraid of flying? Why are they afraid? Do they know how safe flying is statistically? Discuss in a group.

COLLABORATE

D Work in a group. Read the examples in the chart. Then do your own research and complete the chart by listing things that you think seem much more or much less risky than they actually are.

Event	Perceived risk	Actual risk	Supporting data
Plane crashes	High	Low	1 crash for every 7.7 million commercial flights in 2021.
Car crashes	Low	Medium	Kills approx. 1.3 million people every year, or about 3,300 people a day.

E Work with a partner from a different group. Discuss your charts and answer the questions below.

1. Is there anything that surprises you, or that you disagree with?
2. Do you think the data is enough to change how people feel about the things in your charts? Why, or why not?

Checkpoint

Reflect on what you have learned. Check your progress.

I can ... understand and use words related to risk.

aversion	bias	guaranteed	intuition	mental
odds	outcome	phenomenon	probability	rational

 use idioms containing the word *odds*.

 watch and understand a video about irrational decisions.

 write notes about technical terms.

 understand technical terms while listening.

 notice language for helping listeners follow ideas.

 help a listener follow along as I explain a concept.

 collaborate and communicate effectively to identify and explain misunderstood risks.

A skateboarder underneath the Ouse Valley Viaduct, the U.K.

Building Vocabulary

LEARN KEY WORDS

A 🎧 Listen to and read the passage below. Circle **T** for true or **F** for false.

1. Risk-taking in teenagers is a form of self discovery.	T	F
2. Most teenagers take on more risk they can handle.	T	F
3. Most teenagers engage in multiple-risk behavior.	T	F

Risk-Taking and the Teenage Brain

Teenagers are often thought of as **daring**, or even **reckless**. They are known to be big risk-takers: open to new experiences, and unafraid of the **consequences** of their actions. But why exactly are teens wired this way?

For young people, risk-taking is an essential part of growing up. It is a way for teens to learn about themselves. As they **mature** and gain independence, they often seek new and exciting ways to test the boundaries of what they're capable of. They put themselves in unfamiliar situations, try challenging or even dangerous stunts, and—as they succeed or fail—discover new things about themselves that help them better forge their identities.

Risk-taking can obviously be dangerous if it goes too far, but fortunately, most teenagers know where to draw the line. However, there are some who are **prone to** engaging in what's called multiple-risk behavior: they take on more risk than they can handle, and often suffer long-term consequences as a result. These **vulnerable** teens are a minority, but it is nonetheless important that we recognize them and do more to help safeguard their futures.

B Work with a partner. Discuss the questions below.

1. Look at the photo. It shows a young skateboarder performing a stunt at the Ouse Valley Viaduct in the U.K. How risky is the activity he's doing, and why do you think he's doing it?

2. Do you think you take on more risk than other people your age? How often do you think about the potential long-term effects of the risks you take?

C Match the correct form of each word in **bold** in Exercise A with its meaning.

1. _____ the (often negative) effect of an action

2. _____ to grow older and/or wiser

3. _____ likely to do something

4. _____ easily harmed by something

5. _____ brave and willing to try new, sometimes dangerous, things

6. _____ likely to do dangerous things without thinking about what could go wrong

D Read the excerpts from Kashfia Rahman's TED Talk in Lesson F. Circle the meaning of the words in **bold.**

1. " … the teen brain is still in the process of maturation, and this makes them **exceptionally** poor at decision-making, … "

   a. notably more than others   b. occasionally more than others

2. "Habituation explains how our brains **adapt** to some behaviors, like lying, with repeated exposures."

   a. change to suit new conditions   b. protect us from harmful behavior

3. "I took risks realizing that **unforeseen** opportunities often come from risk-taking."

   a. unfortunate   b. unexpected

4. "Can positive risk-taking **escalate** with repeated exposures?"

   a. become less over time   b. become more over time

E The word **mature** has different forms that can be used to talk about many different things. Read the sentences. Circle **V** (verb), **N** (noun), or **A** (adjective).

	V	N	A
1. This cheese is very **mature**, so it's not to everyone's taste.	V	N	A
2. Most animals don't take as long as humans to fully **mature**.	V	N	A
3. She's young, but she's shown a lot of **maturity**.	V	N	A
4. Despite his age, he's still rather **immature**.	V	N	A
5. Their **immaturity** isn't surprising. They've never had to work for anything.	V	N	A
6. Their excitement was **premature**. The event had to be canceled.	V	N	A

COMMUNICATE

F Note an example next to each prompt below. Discuss with a partner.

1. a daring thing that you did
2. a problem that escalated quickly
3. a reckless mistake made by you or someone else
4. someone who's exceptionally good at something
5. an unforeseen consequence of something you did

G The passage in Exercise A talks about risk-taking as a form of self discovery. Discuss with a partner.

1. What are some risks you've taken that have helped you learn more about yourself?
2. Can we learn from both the positive and negative consequences of risk?

Viewing and Note-taking

LEARNING OBJECTIVES

- Watch and understand a talk about teenagers and risk-taking
- Notice the pronunciation of digraphs and consonant clusters

TEDTALKS

In 2017, while she was still in high school, **Kashfia Rahman** won a prestigious award at an international science fair for her research on teenage risk-taking. In her TED Talk, *How Risk-Taking Changes a Teenager's Brain*, Rahman talks about her research, as well as how her own risk-taking made her a stronger, more resilient person.

BEFORE VIEWING

A Read the information about Kashfia Rahman and think about the passage you read in Lesson E about teenage risk-taking. What are some questions you think Rahman's research tried to answer? Discuss with a partner.

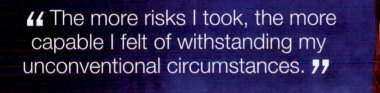

❝ The more risks I took, the more capable I felt of withstanding my unconventional circumstances. **❞**

WHILE VIEWING

B ▶ **LISTEN FOR MAIN IDEAS** Watch Segment 1 of Kashfia Rahman's TED Talk. Complete the notes below.

WHAT SHE NOTICED:

The more risks teens took, _____

_____

WHY WAS THIS?

One explanation was that _____

_____

But this didn't explain why:

– teens are more vulnerable than _____

_____

– not all teens _____

_____

KASHFIA'S THEORY:

Habituation: As teens take more risks, _____

_____

C ▶ **LISTEN FOR DETAILS** Watch Segment 2 of Rahman's talk. Answer the questions.

1. How did Rahman measure people's risk-taking behaviors?

_____

2. What was the purpose of the EEG headset?

_____

3. How did habituation affect people's emotions?

_____

4. What does Rahman say is needed to limit teenage risk-taking?

_____

WORDS IN THE TALK

neuroscientist (n) someone who studies the brain
desensitization (n) becoming less responsive to or affected by something
perfect storm (phr) a set of circumstances where many bad things happen at the same time

D ▶ **LISTEN FOR DETAILS** Watch Segment 3 of Rahman's TED Talk. Discuss the questions below with a partner.

1. Why is it ironic that Rahman's research project taught her to take risks?

2. In what ways did positive risk-taking benefit Rahman?

3. What did Rahman identify as a possible idea for her next research project? How does it relate to her original idea?

AFTER VIEWING

E **SUMMARIZE** Rahman's TED Talk can be divided into six parts. Read the headings and write notes for each part. Then compare notes with a partner.

1 Rahman notices something	2 She begins her research	3 The results are eye-opening
4 She suggests two changes	5 She reflects on her growth	6 She raises a question

PRONUNCIATION *Digraphs and consonant clusters*

F 🎧 Listen to and read the excerpt from the TED Talk. Then look at the bold consonant pairs. Find and underline the digraph.

"This **st**ill image of me experimenti**ng** in my school li**br**ary may seem ordinary, but to me, it re**pr**esents a sort of in**sp**iration."

G Work with a partner. Look at the words in the box and find the pairs or groups of consonants. Are they digraphs or clusters? Do some words have both? Use your ideas to complete the Venn diagram.

children	club	driving	geography
phase	risk	searching	thrill

Words with digraphs   **Words with consonant clusters**

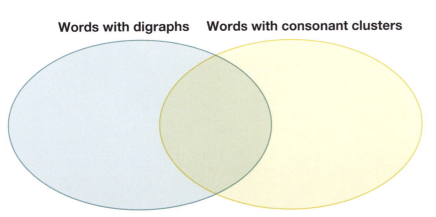

Thinking Critically

ANALYZE INFORMATION

A Look at the three risks below. Which would you be most likely to take? Discuss with a partner.

    a. Quit your job and start your own business.

    b. Quit your job to travel around the world.

    c. Work or study in a country you know little about.

B Look at the infographic and answer the questions. Discuss your answers with a partner.

    1. What do you think the chart is for?

    2. How does the chart work? Write down instructions for using it.

    3. In what situations would the chart be useful?

Is it worth it?

RISK vs. CONSEQUENCES

HIGH

Probability of bad outcome

5	10	15	20	25
4	8	12	16	20
3	6	9	12	15
2	4	6	8	10
1	2	3	4	5

LOW ← → **HIGH**

Impact of bad outcome

A hiker looks out at the city of Matera, in Italy.

C Work with a partner. Look at the three risks in Exercise A. Think of two things that could go wrong for each risk. Then use the infographic in Exercise B to work out a risk value for each outcome.

	Possible bad outcomes	Impact	Probability	Risk value
Risk 1				
Risk 2				
Risk 3				

D 🎧 Listen to a talk about risk and reward. Circle **T** for true or **F** for false.

1. Both the infographic and the talk touch on the consequences of risk-taking.   **T**   **F**

2. Both the infographic and the talk touch on the rewards of risk-taking.   **T**   **F**

3. People are more likely to take big risks if the rewards are high.   **T**   **F**

4. The rewards we get from risk-taking need to be tangible.   **T**   **F**

E Look at the risks in Exercise A. Think of two possible rewards for each situation.

Risk 1 _____   _____

Risk 2 _____   _____

Risk 3 _____   _____

F Work with a partner. Look at your answers in Exercises C and E. Does thinking critically about the consequences and rewards associated with the three risks in Exercise A change how you feel about them? Why, or why not?

COMMUNICATE *Synthesize and evaluate ideas*

G Think about Kashfia Rahman's TED Talk in Lesson F. Discuss the questions below with a partner.

1. Rahman wants to help teens make better decisions about risk. Could the ideas in this lesson help? Why, or why not?

2. Rahman talks about positive risk-taking. How would you define a positive risk, and how could the ideas in this lesson help teens be more open to positive risks?

H In her TED Talk, Rahman talks about policies to limit teenage exposure to negative risks. What might these policies be? How would they work? Discuss with a partner, using ideas from this lesson, and the rest of the unit.

> I wonder if first we need to come up with a list of typical risks?

> That's a good idea. Because we need to think about how to limit each one …

Putting It Together

LEARNING OBJECTIVES

- Research, plan, and present on how risk-taking can be both harmful and beneficial
- Use anecdotes to make presentations more relatable

ASSIGNMENT

Group presentation: Your group is going to give a presentation on how risk-taking can be both beneficial and harmful.

PREPARE

A Review the unit. Discuss with a partner.

1. In what ways are people sometimes illogical when thinking about risks?
2. What do we need to consider in order to assess risk more rationally?

B Work with your group. Think about your lives. What are some risks you took and didn't take? Did you regret taking or not taking these risks? Note down one or two examples for each box below.

RIGHT DECISION	WRONG DECISION
1 Risk I took	**3 Risk I took**
2 Risk I didn't take	**4 Risk I didn't take**

C Plan your presentation. Choose one example from each box in Exercise B and complete the chart below.

	Risk 1	Risk 2	Risk 3	Risk 4
Description				
Potential consequences vs. rewards				
Right decision? Why, or why not?				
Would I do the same thing today?				

D Look back at the vocabulary, pronunciation, and communication skills you've learned in this unit. What can you use in your presentation? Note any useful language below.

_____

_____

_____

E Below are some ways to structure your anecdotes and make them engaging. Think about how you can add details like this to the anecdotes in your presentation.

- Set the scene: describe interesting parts of the where, when and why of your story.

- Explain the problem: describe what you thought and felt.

- Describe the outcome: focus on what was shocking, surprising or interesting.

- Reflect: share what you learned. Can others learn from your experience?

F Practice your presentation. Make use of the presentation skill that you've learned.

PRESENT

G Give your presentation to another group. Watch their presentation and evaluate them using the Presentation Scoring Rubrics at the back of the book.

H Discuss your evaluation with the other group. Give feedback on two things they did well and two areas for improvement.

Checkpoint

Reflect on what you have learned. Check your progress.

I can ... understand and use words related to risky behavior.

adapt	consequence	daring	escalate	exceptionally
mature	prone to	reckless	unforeseen	vulnerable

understand different forms of the word *mature*.

watch and understand a talk about teenagers and risk-taking.

notice the pronunciation of digraphs and consonant clusters.

interpret an infographic about risk assessment.

synthesize and evaluate ideas about risk, consequence, and reward.

use personal anecdotes to make presentations more relatable.

give a presentation on how risk-taking can be both harmful and beneficial.

Diners enjoy Sichuan cuisine at a restaurant in New York, U.S.A.

5

Food for Thought

 **Should we rethink what we eat?**

In the photo, we see a Sichuan hot pot surrounded by various other ingredients. Sichuan cuisine is known for its rich flavors and intense spiciness, which begs the question: would you eat food like this? For most of us, the answer depends on the flavors we prefer or even how health-conscious we are. But should we also consider what impact the food we eat has on the world? In this unit, we'll take a closer look at our diets and explore alternative foods that are good for both us and the planet.

THINK and DISCUSS

1 Look at the photo and read the caption. Do you know where food like this comes from? How do you think it tastes?

2 Look at the essential question and the unit introduction. How does the food we eat impact the planet?

Building Vocabulary

LEARNING OBJECTIVES

• Use ten words related to farming and food
• Understand noun forms of *consume*, *equivalent*, and *harvest*

LEARN KEY WORDS

A 🎧 Listen to and read the information below. What is the main idea?

    a. how global food production and consumption has changed over time

    b. what foods are best for our health and the planet

    c. ways we can increase food production to meet global demands

B Match the correct form of each word in **bold** from the reading with its meaning.

    1. _____ to eat

    2. _____ of equal value

    3. _____ can be eaten

    4. _____ to raise an animal

    5. _____ a lack of something

    6. _____ to pick or gather crops

    7. _____ the practice of farming

    8. _____ animals that are raised for food

    9. _____ a basic food that people often eat

    10. _____ the substances we get from food that keep us healthy

FEEDING THE WORLD

In recent decades, eating habits have changed dramatically both in terms of *what* we eat and *how much*. Because of improved standards of living, we now have access to a more diverse range of foods, from **staples** to less common items. On the one hand, this is good because fewer people are hungry, and vitamin **deficiencies** are rarer. On the other hand, people are generally eating a lot more.

Compared with the 1970s, Earth's population has more than doubled, and people **consume** at least 500 extra calories a day on average—which is roughly **equivalent** to eating an additional large breakfast every day. Furthermore, people are consuming more foods from animals, which require more resources to produce. In fact, almost 40% of the crops we grow are used to **rear** cows and other **livestock** rather than feed people.

There is increasing concern over whether farmers can **harvest** enough **edible** crops so everyone can get the **nutrition** they need. Moreover, the environmental impact of increased **agriculture** is significant. Our growing food needs are linked directly to climate change, and while that may be unwelcome news, it at least raises the possibility that solving the food crisis will help fix our planet.

C Work with a partner. Write the noun form(s) of each word. Use a dictionary if necessary.

1. consume _____ _____

2. equivalent _____ _____ _____

3. harvest _____ _____

D Complete the questions using the words in **bold** from the passage. Then discuss the questions with a partner.

1. In my country, we don't grow many crops because we don't have much land. How important is _____ in your country?

2. What foods do people in your country _____ more of now than before?

3. Do you try to eat healthy food? How important is good _____ to you?

4. Rice is the most widely eaten food in the world. What other _____ foods can you name?

COMMUNICATE

E Work in a group. Discuss the questions.

1. The infographic shows how what we consume is slowly changing. Which of these changes do you think are most worrying, and why?

2. Do you think food consumption will continue to grow at a similar rate? Why, or why not?

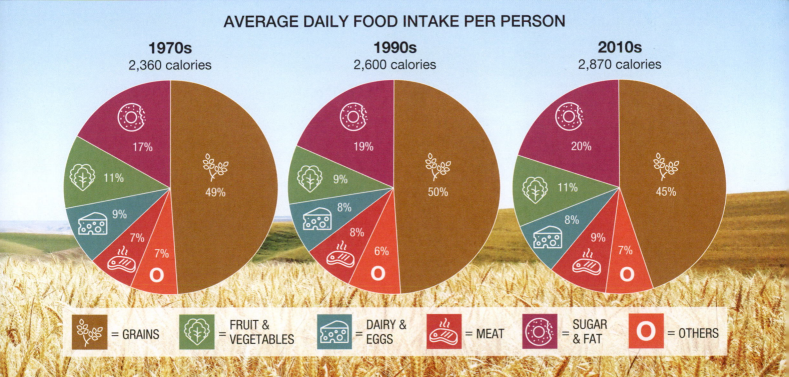

AVERAGE DAILY FOOD INTAKE PER PERSON

1970s
2,360 calories

1990s
2,600 calories

2010s
2,870 calories

1970s: Sugar & Fat 17%, Fruit & Vegetables 11%, Dairy & Eggs 9%, Meat 7%, Others 7%, Grains 49%

1990s: Sugar & Fat 19%, Fruit & Vegetables 9%, Dairy & Eggs 8%, Meat 8%, Others 6%, Grains 50%

2010s: Sugar & Fat 20%, Fruit & Vegetables 11%, Dairy & Eggs 8%, Meat 9%, Others 7%, Grains 45%

= GRAINS   = FRUIT & VEGETABLES   = DAIRY & EGGS   = MEAT   = SUGAR & FAT   O = OTHERS

Viewing and Note-taking

LEARNING OBJECTIVES

- Watch a video about eating insects
- Notice time references
- Recognize persuasive language

BEFORE VIEWING

A You are going to watch a TED-Ed video about eating insects. Read these ideas from the video. How much do you agree with each idea, on a scale from 1 (strongly disagree) to 5 (strongly agree)?

1. People are generally disgusted by the prospect of cooking and eating insects.   1 2 3 4 5

2. Entomophagy, or eating insects, could be a cost-effective way to feed the planet.   1 2 3 4 5

3. Bugs can be a delicious source of nutrition if they're prepared well.   1 2 3 4 5

4. Farming insects has less of an environmental impact than farming livestock.   1 2 3 4 5

B In the photo, a visitor to the 2018 International Green Week trade fair in Berlin is about to try burger patties made from ground buffalo worms—a type of insect that is growing in popularity as a food source. Discuss the questions below with a partner.

1. Would you consider trying a burger like this?
2. Do you think that insect burgers can taste as good as regular burgers?

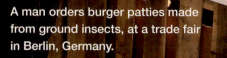

A man orders burger patties made from ground insects, at a trade fair in Berlin, Germany.

WHILE VIEWING

C ▶ **LISTEN FOR MAIN IDEAS** Watch the TED-Ed video about eating insects and circle the main idea.

a. Throughout history, people have eaten insects.

b. Eating insects is good for us and the planet.

c. Insects are an important food source for many people.

D ▶ **LISTEN FOR TIME REFERENCES** Work with a partner and try to match the ideas below to the correct time. Then watch again and check your answers.

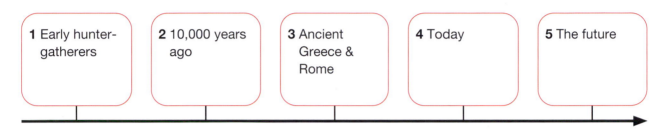

| 1 Early hunter-gatherers | 2 10,000 years ago | 3 Ancient Greece & Rome | 4 Today | 5 The future |

a. Agriculture starts in the Middle East.

b. Attitudes to eating insects change.

c. Farming insects could help people in developing countries.

d. Humans learn insects can be eaten.

e. Insects are considered a luxury snack.

f. People think of insects as irritating.

g. Two billion people consume insects.

E ▶ **LISTEN FOR PERSUASIVE LANGUAGE** Watch some excerpts from the video. Write the tone of the speaker's voice (positive, negative, or neutral), as well as any positive or negative words that stood out.

Excerpt	Tone	Positive/Negative words
1		
2		
3		
4		
5		

AFTER VIEWING

F **REFLECT** Work in a group. Look again at your answers in Exercises A and B. Have your views changed now that you've watched the video? Why, or why not?

> I would never have considered eating insects before. Now I'm curious!

Noticing Language

LISTEN FOR LANGUAGE   *Use qualifiers and intensifiers*

A Read the phrases in the box below. Discuss the questions with a partner. Then think of examples of how you could use each expression as a qualifier or intensifier.

Which word or expression would you use to:

1. strengthen the idea you're expressing?

2. describe things that are likely to be true?

3. describe things that you are less sure about?

4. present other people's opinions or findings?

5. compare something with another thing?

> **Communication Skill**
> **Using Qualifiers and Intensifiers**
>
> Qualifiers and intensifiers are words or phrases that change the meaning of another word, phrase, or idea. You can use them to make an opinion seem more or less certain, or to make an idea sound stronger or weaker.

apparently	possible	relatively
might	probably	many believe
may not	highly	some people say
often	according to	research suggests

B 🎧 Listen to four excerpts from the TED-Ed video in Lesson B. Write the qualifiers and intensifiers from Exercise A that you hear, and note down why you think the speaker used them.

Intensifier/Qualifier   Reason

1. _____*probably*_____   *The story is likely to be true, but it's impossible to be completely sure.*

2. _____   _____

3. _____   _____

4. _____   _____

_____   _____

C 🎧 Listen to three short talks. Complete the sentences with the words you hear. Then check with a partner. What other words from Exercise A can you use to complete the sentences?

1. The idea of eating insects makes many people uncomfortable. However, it's _____ to turn certain bugs into flour that can be used to make foods like bread or pasta. Because consumers would never see the insects, powders like these _____ make the idea of eating bugs more appealing.

2. Aquaponics combines farming fish and growing plants in a single system. The nutrient-rich water in which the fish are raised is used to grow plants, too. _____ that aquaponics will help humans meet our food needs in a way that's sustainable and _____ eco-friendly.

3. A common misconception is that farmers can't produce enough food for everyone, but that _____ be true. According to studies, about a third of the food farmers produce is lost before it reaches consumers. If we can reduce this food waste, we'd _____ have enough food for everyone.

D 🎧 Listen to a talk about the DASH diet and follow along using the outline below. Check (✓) the points the speaker qualifies. What qualifying language from Exercise B does the speaker use?

> ### The DASH Diet
> ☐ Little known but best diet:
> > ☐ eat veg/fruit/whole grains/low-fat dairy/lean protein/nuts
> > ☐ avoid fatty foods/processed foods/salt
>
> ☐ DASH designed to treat high blood pressure:
> > ☐ a serious and increasingly common condition
> > ☐ DASH diet treats condition effectively
>
> ☐ DASH has other benefits:
> > ☐ people lose weight
> > ☐ prevents Alzheimer's disease (a serious brain condition)

COMMUNICATE

E Think of two foods: one you think people should eat more and one they should eat less. Prepare notes below. Include reasons and benefits for each recommendation. Finally, consider which points you need to qualify.

> Eat more of this: _____
>
> Reasons and benefits:

> Eat less of this: _____
>
> Reasons and benefits:

F Work with a partner. Share your recommendations from Exercise E, and ask follow-up questions. Use qualifiers when necessary.

UNIT
5

A B
C D

Communicating Ideas

ASSIGNMENT

Task: You are going to collaborate in a group to express ideas about how you think a new and unusual kind of restaurant should be run.

LISTEN FOR INFORMATION

A 🎧 **LISTEN FOR MAIN IDEAS** Listen to a talk. Which option best summarizes it?

   a. A chef is trying to persuade people to visit his new restaurant.

   b. A chef is trying to find out what people think about his idea for a restaurant.

   c. An entrepreneur is trying to convince a group of chefs to work in his restaurant.

B 🎧 **LISTEN FOR DETAILS** Listen again. Complete the focus group handout below. Compare answers with a partner.

Our four goals

1 _____   3 _____

2 _____   4 _____

Why insects?

• _____

• _____

• _____

• _____

• _____

What do you think?

• General concept   • _____

• Menu and _____   • Tips and suggestions

C Imagine you are participants in the focus group discussion. Complete the feedback form below. Then discuss your answers with a partner.

FEEDBACK FORM   (1 = strongly disagree, 5 = strongly agree)

1. I care about the environmental impact of my food.   1 2 3 4 5

2. I am concerned about eating too much meat.   1 2 3 4 5

3. I like the concept of the restaurant.   1 2 3 4 5

4. I think a restaurant like this could be popular.   1 2 3 4 5

COLLABORATE

D Work with a partner. Imagine you're starting your own insect-based restaurant.
Note down ideas for the restaurant in the chart below.

Feature menu items		Theme and design
_____		_____
_____		_____
_____	**Restaurant name ideas**	_____
	_____	
	_____	
Target customers	_____	Other suggestions
_____		_____
_____		_____
_____		_____

E Work in a group. Discuss your ideas from Exercise D. Provide feedback on each
other's ideas, and use qualifiers and intensifiers when necessary.

What do you think about insect burgers?

That's probably a good idea. Apparently, some taste just like regular burgers.

Checkpoint

Reflect on what you have learned. Check your progress.

I can ... ☐ understand and use words related to farming and food.

agriculture	consume	deficiency	edible	equivalent
harvest	livestock	nutrition	rear	staple

☐ use noun forms of *consume, equivalent,* and *harvest.*

☐ watch and understand a video about eating insects.

☐ notice time references when taking notes.

☐ listen for persuasive language.

☐ notice language for qualifying and intensifying statements.

☐ use qualifiers and intensifiers to explain why some foods might be good or bad for you.

☐ collaborate and communicate effectively to give feedback on a new kind of restaurant.

A scientist presents a genetically modified variety of rice during a press tour in the Philippines.

UNIT 5
E F G H

Building Vocabulary

LEARN KEY WORDS

A Work with a partner. Discuss the questions below.

1. Look at the photos on the right. How often do you eat these foods? Do you consider them healthy? Why, or why not?

2. The photo on the left shows a genetically modified strain of rice called "golden rice." Are you happy to eat genetically modified foods? Why, or why not?

B 🎧 Listen to and read the passage below. Does the information in the passage change any of your answers in Exercise A? Why, or why not?

Modified Foods

When we think about food production, we usually think of farms and fields—not laboratories. Yet many important food innovations have been the result of human **ingenuity** and scientific research. Still, food modification remains controversial—even though it has long been crucial to our success as a species.

Since ancient times, humans have selectively bred crops and animals to create new breeds with more desirable traits. And over long spans of time, this has drastically altered many plant and animal species. In recent times, we've learned to fast-forward this process by modifying food at a **cellular** level, and this has led to amazing **breakthroughs**. For example, the IR8 strain of rice produces harvests that are ten times bigger, which has led to social **transformation** in countries like India and the Philippines. Another rice variety—golden rice—has the potential to save millions of children from blindness every year.

Many people are understandably concerned about food modification. After all, not all food innovations have been positive. Ultra-processed foods, for example, are linked to several major health issues. Yet, in this rapidly changing world, food modification has the potential to help us meet our food needs and **alleviate** human **suffering**. Perhaps the best approach is to be both cautious and open to the potential of food modification.

C Match the correct form of each word in **bold** from Exercise B with its meaning.

1. _____ pain or severe discomfort over a prolonged period

2. _____ a complete change that improves someone or something

3. _____ an important discovery or event that significantly changes a situation

4. _____ the ability to come up with clever new ideas or inventions

5. _____ to make something less severe or less difficult

6. _____ relating to microscopic parts of plants and animals

D Read the summary of a part of Isha Datar's TED Talk in Lesson F. Match the words in **bold** to their definitions.

Cellular agriculture refers to the growing of meat in a lab. Scientists **extract** animal cells and grow them in a **stable** environment. This stability is crucial as the cells cannot develop or **flourish** if the temperature or pressure changes. Cellular agriculture has many benefits. It is far better for the environment than normal animal farming, and it requires much less land, allowing countries to **restore** forests previously cut down for farming. Most notably, it does not involve the killing of animals.

1. _____ unlikely to change

2. _____ to grow well

3. _____ to return something to its original condition

4. _____ to take out or remove

E Work with a partner. Scan the passage in Exercise B.

1. Find a synonym for the word *breakthrough*. _____

2. Find four adjectives that collocate with *breakthrough* and its synonym in Question 1.

i_____   r_____

s_____   m_____

COMMUNICATE

F Note an example next to each prompt below. Discuss with a partner.

1. a time you or someone you know demonstrated ingenuity _____

2. a breakthrough that has had positive and negative effects _____

3. a period of transformation in your country's history _____

4. old items that people often restore _____

G Write down in the chart some food items you frequently eat. Discuss with a partner.

1. How natural or processed are they? Write their numbers on the scale below.
2. Do you think you consume too much processed food? Why, or why not?
3. How easy would it be to replace the processed foods you eat with more natural options?

Breakfast	Lunch	Dinner
1 _____	4 _____	7 _____
2 _____	5 _____	8 _____
3 _____	6 _____	9 _____

◄————┼————┼————┼————┼————┼————┼————┼————┼————►

natural   **processed**

Viewing and Note-taking

LEARNING OBJECTIVES

- Watch and understand a talk about the benefits of lab-grown meat
- Use stress and emphasis in numerical expressions

TEDTALKS

Isha Datar is an expert in cellular agriculture—a term she invented to describe growing meat from cells rather than raising whole animals for meat. In her TED Talk, *How We Could Eat Real Meat Without Harming Animals*, she explains what cellular agriculture is, how it works, and why it could benefit people, animals, and the planet.

BEFORE VIEWING

A Read the information above about Isha Datar. Discuss with a partner.

1. How is cellular agriculture similar to and different from modifying food in a lab?

2. What are some possible benefits of cellular agriculture?

> **"** … I think it's our once-in-a-lifetime opportunity to get a second chance at agriculture, to do things better, and to learn from our mistakes. **"**

WHILE VIEWING

B ▶ **LISTEN FOR MAIN IDEAS** Watch Segment 1 of Isha Datar's TED Talk and take notes. Then check (✓) the things that Isha Datar does.

1. ☐ She defines what cellular agriculture is.

2. ☐ She explains how cellular agriculture works.

3. ☐ She describes the flavor of lab-grown meat.

4. ☐ She talks about the popularity of lab-grown meat.

5. ☐ She mentions some benefits of cellular agriculture.

C ▶ **LISTEN FOR DETAILS** Work with a partner. Watch Segment 1 again. Complete the flow chart.

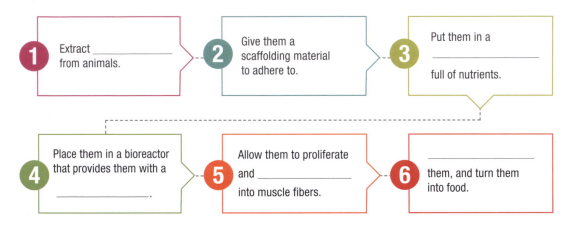

1 Extract _____ from animals.

2 Give them a scaffolding material to adhere to.

3 Put them in a _____ full of nutrients.

4 Place them in a bioreactor that provides them with a _____.

5 Allow them to proliferate and _____ into muscle fibers.

6 _____ them, and turn them into food.

D ▶ **LISTEN FOR DETAILS** Watch Segment 2 of Datar's TED Talk. Answer the questions.

1. How long does a broiler live before it is killed for its meat? _____

2. What proportion of pigs on Earth have died from African swine fever? _____

3. What percentage of greenhouse gases are produced just by cows? _____

4. What percentage of Earth's land is used to raise food for livestock? _____

5. How much less land does Isha Datar say is needed for cellular agriculture? _____

E ▶ **INFER** Watch Segment 3 of Datar's TED Talk. Which statements do you think Datar would probably agree with? Circle **Y** for yes or **N** for no.

1. We should all stop eating meat and animal-based foods. **Y** **N**

2. Meat and animal-based foods are rich and flavorful. **Y** **N**

3. We already have the means to completely replace farming with cellular agriculture. **Y** **N**

4. Cellular agriculture will help us meet our increasing food needs. **Y** **N**

5. Meat from cellular agriculture won't taste as good as meat from animals. **Y** **N**

WORDS IN THE TALK
advocate (n) somebody who publicly supports an idea or plan
scaffolding (n) a structure that supports something
subsistence (n) living completely off the food one grows

AFTER VIEWING

F **REFLECT** Work in a group. Discuss the questions.

1. Would you eat meat grown from cells in a lab? Why, or why not?

2. Read the quotation below. How does this sound to you? Which ideas would you be interested in trying? Which would you not be interested in trying? Why?

> "But if we can grow meat from cells, suddenly the boundaries for what meat can be will totally change. Meat could be thin and translucent. It could be liquid. It could be crunchy. It could be bubbly."

PRONUNCIATION *Stress and emphasis in numerical expressions*

G 🎧 Listen to these numerical expressions from the TED Talk. If the numbers and nouns are stressed similarly, write **N** for neutral. If a particular number is emphasized, circle it.

1. six to eight weeks

2. 99 percent less land

3. hundreds of millions of pigs

4. about a third of this planet

5. some 12,000 years ago

> **Pronunciation Skill**
>
> **Stress and Emphasis in Numerical Expressions**
>
> Numerical expressions typically include numbers and nouns. The nouns may be units of measurement like *dollars* or *years*. In a neutral sentence, a speaker will typically stress both the number and the noun. But sometimes a speaker will choose to emphasize either the number or the noun so it stands out for the listener.

H Answer these questions. Then interview several classmates and note the numerical expressions they use in their responses. Then work in a group to discuss your results, emphasizing numbers or units as necessary. What results were the most interesting? Why?

1. How many meals and snacks do you eat on average every day?

2. Generally speaking, what percentage of your meals do you cook and eat at home?

3. In a typical month, how much money do you spend on food? What proportion of that do you spend at restaurants?

A scientist runs tests on meat grown in a lab.

Thinking Critically

ANALYZE INFORMATION

A Look at the infographic and answer the questions. Discuss your answers with a partner.

1. How many groups of people are involved in putting chicken on people's tables?
2. What other stages and people do you think have been omitted?

CHICKEN The Journey from Farm to Table

Chicken is the most popular source of protein in the world, accounting for more than 40% of meat consumption globally. Relative to other meats, it is a low-cost and healthy option, which is why demand for it has risen sharply over the last few decades. But what does it take to supply the world with so much chicken? The journey from farm to table is today a highly industrialized process that involves millions of people.

Chickens are …

1. raised by farmers
2. checked for diseases
3. slaughtered
4. cleaned and inspected
5. cut and packed
6. delivered to stores
7. purchased and consumed

B 🎧 Listen to a talk about the meat industry and take notes. What does the speaker say? Use your notes to correct one mistake in each statement. Then discuss with a partner.

1. Traditional farming uses too much water, causes too much pollution, requires too much land, and produces too much food.

2. Cellular agriculture could massively disrupt the meat industry and result in huge intended consequences.

3. If animal farming became unprofitable, it would be inexpensive for animal farmers to switch to crop farming or cellular agriculture.

COMMUNICATE   *Synthesize and evaluate ideas*

C Work with a partner. Who expresses the ideas below: the speaker you just heard, Isha Datar, or both? Write the numbers (1–4) in the Venn diagram.

1. Traditional meat production has a number of issues.

2. Cellular agriculture will help us meet our food needs.

3. Traditional meat farming benefits many people in society.

4. Solutions to issues can lead to unexpected consequences.

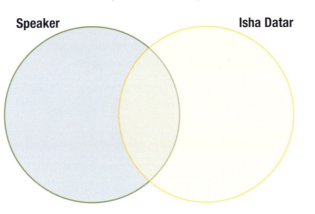

Speaker   **Isha Datar**

D Work in a group. Look at the infographic and your answers in Exercise A. Who would be most negatively affected by cellular agriculture? List the top five groups, and circle how badly you think they would be affected (1 = slightly, 10 = severely).

1. _____   1   2   3   4   5   6   7   8   9   10

2. _____   1   2   3   4   5   6   7   8   9   10

3. _____   1   2   3   4   5   6   7   8   9   10

4. _____   1   2   3   4   5   6   7   8   9   10

5. _____   1   2   3   4   5   6   7   8   9   10

E In your groups, weigh the benefits of replacing traditional meat farming with something like cellular agriculture against the downsides. What do you think is the right thing to do, and why?

> I think the benefits definitely outweigh the downsides, but …

Putting It Together

ASSIGNMENT

Group presentation: Your group is going to give a presentation on a possible solution to one aspect of the food crisis.

PREPARE

A Review the unit. What is the food crisis, and what are its causes? Discuss with a partner.

_____

_____

B Work with your group. Choose a solution below to help address an aspect of the food crisis. Research your solution, and note down useful information.

- Encourage people to eat less meat
- Farm new crops (e.g., seaweed)
- Reduce the amount of food wasted
- Make agriculture more efficient
- Your own idea

_____

_____

_____

C Plan your presentation. Make notes in the chart below.

Question	Notes
What is the solution and how would it help?	
What challenges exist in implementing the solution?	
How can these challenges be overcome or reduced?	
How does the solution compare to either eating insects _or_ cellular agriculture?	

D Look back at the vocabulary, pronunciation, and communication skills you've learned in this unit. What can you use in your presentation? Note any useful language below.

_____

_____

_____

_____

E Below are some questions to help you find relatable elements in your presentation. Where can you make use of your answers in your talk?

Who is my audience?	What would interest them most?
What do they know?	What would benefit them most?
How do they feel about the topic?	What do I have in common with them?

Presentation Skill

Make Your Presentation Relatable

In her TED Talk, Isha Datar talks about her own love of meat and the new flavors she wants to try. She does this to make her talk relatable. To make your presentation relatable, consider what your audience knows and is interested in.

F Practice your presentation. Make use of the presentation skill that you've learned.

PRESENT

G Give your presentation to another group. Watch their presentation and evaluate them using the Presentation Scoring Rubrics at the back of the book.

H Discuss your evaluation with the other group. Give feedback on two things they did well and two areas for improvement.

Checkpoint

Reflect on what you have learned. Check your progress.

I can ... ☐ understand and use words related to scientific food innovations.

| alleviate | breakthrough | cellular | extract | flourish |
| ingenuity | restore | stable | suffering | transformation |

☐ use synonyms and collocations of _breakthrough_.
☐ watch and understand a talk about the benefits of lab-grown meat.
☐ notice the use of stress and emphasis in numerical expressions.
☐ interpret an infographic about the meat industry.
☐ synthesize and evaluate ideas about switching to meat alternatives.
☐ make my presentation relatable.
☐ give a presentation on a solution to an aspect of the food crisis.

6

Hooked on Our Phones?

Q Do we use our phones too much?

Our phones are amazing devices, but do we use them too much? The street sign in the photo was put up by two Swedish artists precisely for that reason. Its purpose was to remind pedestrians to look up from their phones before crossing the street. In this unit, we'll explore the issues of phone usage and addiction, and consider whether smartphones are doing us more harm than good.

A street sign in Stockholm, Sweden.

THINK and DISCUSS

1 Look at the photo and read the caption. Do you think the sign in the photo is effective? Why, or why not?

2 Look at the essential question and the unit introduction. How much do you use your phone? Do you think you're hooked on your phone?

Building Vocabulary

LEARN KEY WORDS

A 🎧 Listen to and read the information below. Discuss the questions with a partner.

1. What are some of the things smartphones have replaced?
2. Which mobile phone milestone do you think was most significant?
3. Which of the phone functions mentioned in the article do you think is most useful?

MOBILE PHONE MILESTONES

Mobile phones **empower** billions around the world. They allow people to do many things that would have been difficult or impossible to do in the past. They've become so **widespread** and central to our lives, in fact, that we often forget just how lucky we are to have them.

From a historical **perspective**, mobile phone technology has come a long way in a short time. It's hard to imagine that the pocket-sized gadgets we have today started off in 1973 as a bulky machine that did just one thing. Fast forward a few decades though and things get exciting very quickly.

Phones double up as gaming devices, music players, and cameras. They connect to the internet and function as mini computers. They sync up with other **gadgets** like speakers and TVs. They replace books and maps. And we use them to get work done, create art, and even find love.

These days, there's not much we can't do on a good mobile phone—which begs the question: what does the future of these **versatile** devices look like? It's hard to imagine, but whichever direction things go, one thing is for sure: phones aren't getting any less popular than they are today.

1970

1973
The first mobile phone call is made. The phone weighed about 2.5 pounds.

EARLY 1980s
The first mobile phones go on sale. Each one cost $4,000.

MID 1990s
Phones are able to send SMS text messages. The first mobile phone games are introduced.

LATE 1990s
Color screens are introduced. The first color screen displayed just four colors.

EARLY 2000s
Phones are able to connect to the internet. They start to replace cameras and music players.

2007
The age of the smartphone kicks off. Touchscreens replace dial pads and keyboards.

2010s
Smartphones take over and become all-in-one multimedia devices.

TODAY

B Match the correct form of each word in **bold** in Exercise A with its meaning.

1. _____ a device that is usually electronic

2. _____ used or shared by many people

3. _____ to enable people to do something

4. _____ having many uses or skills

5. _____ a point of view, or a way of looking at something

C Read the definitions. Then complete the passage below with the correct forms of the words in **bold**.

addiction	a harmful activity that's hard to stop doing
adversely	in a negative way
excessive	more than is necessary or healthy
diminish	to make something less
nuanced	complex, with subtle differences between different views

Many people think that our phone usage is ¹_____. It ²_____

impacts our health, reduces our attention span, and ³_____ our creativity. Some even

call phone usage a widespread ⁴_____. But others think that the issue is more

⁵_____ than that. We need to consider how and why people use their phones,

as well as what they get out of it.

D Complete the sentences using the correct form of the noun **addict**.

addict	addiction	addictive	addicted

1. He really enjoys this TV show, but I wouldn't call him a TV _____.

2. Some videos games are hard to stop playing. They're really _____.

3. Stan loves coffee a lot, but he doesn't think of it as an _____.

4. She's on social media all the time. She's completely _____ to it!

COMMUNICATE

E Note an example next to each prompt below. Discuss with a partner.

1. an action or event that affected you adversely   _____

2. an activity that someone you know does excessively   _____

3. a gadget you have that is no longer useful   _____

4. a movie, book, or story that you found empowering   _____

5. someone you know who is very versatile   _____

F Work with a partner. Discuss the questions below.

1. What other gadgets or devices not mentioned in the article have phones replaced?

2. What are some ways mobile phones have empowered people around the world?

Viewing and Note-taking

LEARNING OBJECTIVES

• Watch a video podcast about phone addiction
• Notice questions in a talk
• Recognize a speaker's purpose

BEFORE VIEWING

A How much time would someone have to spend on their phone for you to consider them a phone addict? Discuss with a partner.

WHILE VIEWING

B ▶ **LISTEN FOR MAIN IDEAS** Watch Segment 1 of a video podcast about phone addiction. Check the statements you think the speaker would agree with.

1. ☐ Books are probably just as harmful as phones.

2. ☐ People use their phones a lot.

2. ☐ Something is only really an addiction if it causes harm.

4. ☐ Most people are probably addicted to their phones.

C ▶ **LISTEN FOR QUESTIONS** Read the questions below. Then watch Segment 1 again. Summarize what the speaker says after asking each question.

> **Note-taking Skill**
> **Noticing Questions**
>
> When a speaker asks questions, make detailed notes about the responses you hear. This is because questions often signpost new ideas, key details, or what the speaker will discuss next. They outline how the talk is organized.

1. "But are these pocket-sized gadgets really a problem?"

_____

_____

2. "But what if … the small rectangular object … were a book instead?"

_____

_____

3. "Why does one feel OK, but the other feel like an addiction?"

_____

_____

D **INFER** Match the questions in Exercise C with the reason the speaker asks them.

1. _____ "But are these pocket-sized gadgets really a problem?"

2. _____ "But what if … the small rectangular object … were a book instead?"

3. _____ "Why does one feel OK, but the other feel like an addiction?"

a. to introduce the main idea of the talk

b. to explain what it really means to be addicted

c. to show that addiction isn't simply doing something a lot

E ▶ **LISTEN FOR PURPOSE** Watch Segment 2 of the video podcast. Then answer the questions.

1. Why does the speaker list so many different phone functions?

   a. to explain why people use their phones so much

   b. to show how addicted we are to our phones

2. Why does the speaker ask, "Does addiction really explain why we use our phones so much?"

   a. to show how little we understand about phone addiction

   b. to show that heavy phone usage is not the same as phone addiction

3. Why does the speaker bring up history and different technological advancements?

   a. to warn us not to make the same mistakes we made in the past

   b. to show that we used to feel the same way about other technologies

4. What is the speaker's overall purpose?

   a. to show how common phone addiction is   **b.** to challenge the idea of phone addiction

> **Listening Skill**
>
> **Recognizing a Speaker's Purpose**
>
> Speakers typically have a reason for giving a talk. This is their overall purpose. However, different parts of a talk can also have sub-purposes that serve to reinforce the overall purpose. While speakers sometimes state these purposes directly, you will often have to infer them. When listening, think about why the speaker brings up different points and how each point supports the overall purpose.

AFTER VIEWING

F **REFLECT** Work with a partner. Discuss the questions below.

1. Look at your answers in Exercise A. Do you still feel the same way after watching the video?
2. The speaker compares phones to books, and later to radio, TV, and video games. Do you think phones are more harmful than these other things? Why, or why not?
3. In the talk, the speaker asks, "Are we all really addicted to our phones?" What is your view?

> Most people are probably not addicted to their phones, but maybe a small percentage is …

> Personally, I think we are addicted to our phones. Just try going a day without it and see how you feel …

Many people find it hard to put their phones away at night.

UNIT
6
A B C D

Noticing Language

LISTEN FOR LANGUAGE *Describe time, frequency, and duration*

A Work with a partner. Read the phrases below. Add them to the correct column in the chart.

briefly	after I've finished	for about
recently	a short while later	for almost
regularly	three weeks ago	every so often
around the time	occasionally	(twice) a year

> **Communication Skill**
> **Describing Time, Frequency, and Duration**
>
> Adverbials are words, phrases, or clauses that act as adverbs. You can use time adverbials to say *when* something happened, frequency adverbials to say *how often*, and duration adverbials to say *how long*.

Time (when)	Frequency (how often)	Duration (how long)

B 🎧 Complete the sentences from the talk in Lesson B using the expressions below. Then listen to the excerpts from the talk to check your answers. The first one has been done for you.

times a day	~~all the time~~	**hundreds of years ago**
many years later	**every day**	**once every four minutes**

1. "We see headlines _____*all the time*_____ telling us that mobile phone addiction is widespread—that it's something we need to be worried about."

2. "Picture in your mind a teenager who spends many hours _____ looking at a small, rectangular object."

3. "They check their phones about 340 _____. That's about _____!"

4. "_____, when the printing press was invented, people panicked about the destructive effects books and the ideas they contained would have on society. The same fear and anxiety returned _____, when radios became popular ..."

C 🎧 Listen to a talk about pagers. Complete the sentences using the expressions you hear.

1. _____ two decades, … people carried a different sort of mobile telecommunications device in their pockets.

2. You'd see them everywhere … . And you'd hear them go off _____ …

3. To page someone, you had to dial a number and … type in a call-back number before pressing the "pound" key. _____, the person receiving the page would hear a beep …

4. But that was all _____ that mobile phones started to become popular.

D Complete the sentences below so that they are true for you. Share your answers with a partner.

1. I love _____. I do it _____ times a _____.

2. I remember when I _____. Many years later, I still _____
_____.

3. I _____ all the time. After I've finished, _____
_____.

4. Every year, around the time when _____,
I always _____.

5. Every so often, whenever I'm feeling bored, _____
_____.

E Work with a partner. Read the description on the right and guess what it refers to. Then write your own descriptions, using the expressions from Exercises A and B. Can your partner guess what you're describing?

> I do this once or twice a week when my fridge looks empty. I might go to the bank before I do this, and I might spend time in the kitchen after I've finished.

COMMUNICATE

F Follow these steps:

1. Choose one of the topics below, and make notes for a short talk, including some adverbials.

2. Work with a partner. Each person should speak for two minutes about their topic and then answer any follow-up questions.

 a vacation you once took

a place you used to live in

 a phone you used to have

 a job or course you once did

Communicating Ideas

LEARNING OBJECTIVES

• Use appropriate language for talking about time, frequency, and duration
• Collaborate to compare different people's phone usage

ASSIGNMENT

Task: You are going to collaborate in a group to learn about and discuss your cell phone habits.

LISTEN FOR INFORMATION

A 🎧 **LISTEN FOR MAIN IDEAS** Listen to three people describing how they use their phones. Who do you think uses their phone the most? Whose phone usage would you consider the most concerning?

B 🎧 **LISTEN FOR DETAILS** The pie charts show Naomi, Ruben, and Sasha's weekly phone usage. Listen again and write their names below the charts (**1–3**). Then, write the missing activities (**a–c**). Finally, calculate their total weekly phone usage.

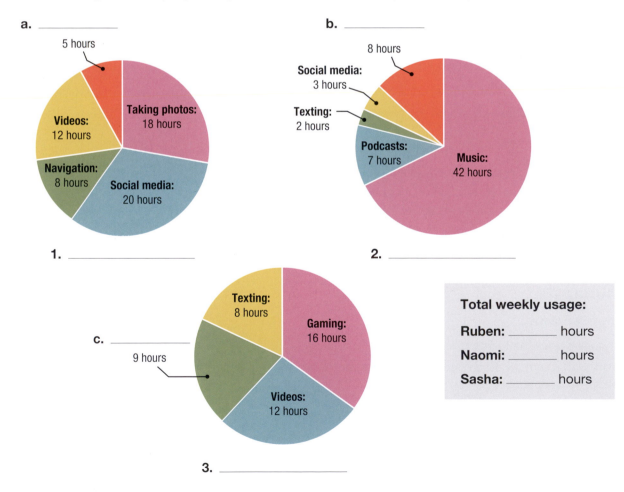

a. _____

5 hours

Videos: 12 hours

Taking photos: 18 hours

Navigation: 8 hours

Social media: 20 hours

1. _____

b. _____

8 hours

Social media: 3 hours

Texting: 2 hours

Podcasts: 7 hours

Music: 42 hours

2. _____

c. _____

9 hours

Texting: 8 hours

Gaming: 16 hours

Videos: 12 hours

3. _____

Total weekly usage:

Ruben: _____ hours

Naomi: _____ hours

Sasha: _____ hours

C Look at the information in Exercise B. Are your answers to the questions in Exercise A still the same? Why, or why not? Discuss with a partner.

COLLABORATE

D Work individually. Write down the top five ways you use your phone. Then estimate how many hours you spend doing each thing per week, and how many additional hours you spend doing other things on your phone. Finally, use the information to draw a pie chart about your phone usage, and calculate your total screen time.

Activity   **Hours per week**

1. _____   _____

2. _____   _____

3. _____   _____

4. _____   _____

5. _____   _____

6. Others   _____

TOTAL: _____

E Work in groups. Discuss your pie charts. Then look at Naomi, Ruben, and Sasha's pie charts. Discuss the questions below.

1. How similar is your group's phone usage to the people in Exercise A?

2. Should Naomi, Ruben, or Sasha be concerned about their phone usage?

3. Is anyone from your group concerned about their own phone usage? If so, why?

> Ruben uses his phone a lot, but I don't think he needs to be concerned because ...

> I was a bit shocked to see how much time I spend on games per week ...

Checkpoint

Reflect on what you have learned. Check your progress.

I can ... ☐ understand and use words related to phone usage and addiction.

addiction	adversely	diminish	empower	excessive
gadget	nuanced	perspective	versatile	widespread

☐ use different forms of the word *addict*.

☐ watch and understand a talk about phone addiction.

☐ notice questions and use them to organize my notes.

☐ recognize a speaker's purpose.

☐ notice language for describing time, frequency, and duration.

☐ use adverbials to talk about a past experience.

☐ collaborate and communicate effectively to compare different people's phone usage.

A visitor to the Taj Mahal, India, takes selfies using not one, but two phones.

Building Vocabulary

LEARN KEY WORDS

A 🎧 Listen to and read the passage below. Discuss with a partner.

1. Why are phone cameras giving actual cameras "a run for their money"?

2. Why are some photographers concerned about phone cameras?

How Phones Are Changing Photography

I know a food photographer who almost never carries a camera with him. Why? Because the camera on his phone does a good enough job most of the time. It's smaller, plus he can edit his photos as soon as he's taken them. Phone cameras have gotten so powerful that they're giving actual cameras— devices built **solely** for taking photographs—a real run for their money.

While camera phones definitely have their **limitations**, it's hard to argue against how incredibly convenient they are. But is this convenience ruining photography by making it too easy? Some **committed** photographers seem to think so. The art of photography, they say, is getting lost under layers of digital filters and editing. Furthermore, with the sheer number of photos people take on their phones, getting that one **compelling** image is no longer a matter of skill or patience: it's a game of chance.

Still, does any of that really matter? Are smartphones making photography less meaningful, or are they giving opportunities to people who otherwise would not have had them? Phone cameras are only going to get better, and the **impulse** to snap away is only going to grow stronger. Whether this is good or bad for photography is largely down to perspective.

B Work with a partner. Discuss the questions below.

1. Do you usually take photos with your phone or with an actual camera? Why?

2. Do you think smartphones have changed photography? If so, how?

3. Look at the photo. It shows a tourist taking selfies outside the Taj Mahal in India. How do you feel about selfies? How often do you take them?

C Match the correct form of each word in **bold** from Exercise A with its meaning.

1. _____ limitation

2. _____ committed

3. _____ compelling

4. _____ solely

5. _____ impulse

a. only, not involving anything else

b. loyal and dedicated to something

c. a sudden, strong desire to do something

d. powerful and able to hold attention

e. a weakness or disadvantage

D Read the excerpts from Erin Sullivan's TED Talk in Lesson F. Then match the correct form of words in **bold** to their definitions.

> "Sometimes, I visit a popular **landmark**—this one is Horseshoe Bend in Arizona—and I see all the people with their phones and cameras out …"
>
> "I noticed myself feeling pressure and a certain **obligation** to take the camera with me, when sometimes I just wanted the pure experience itself."
>
> "What if you were not allowed to take any pictures at all? Would it feel like a limitation? Or would it feel like a **relief**?"
>
> "I was on a boat with four other photographers, and we were all having our minds blown at the same time, in such close **proximity** to these animals."
>
> "Being eye to eye with these bears gave me a feeling of connection that **transcends** words, and having my camera with me in this case enhanced that."

1. _____ to go beyond limitations
2. _____ happiness when a bad experience ends or is avoided
3. _____ a famous or easily recognizable place
4. _____ nearness
5. _____ a sense of responsibility or duty to do something

E The words in the box collocate with *compelling*. Complete the sentences using the most suitable words.

argument	evidence	reason	account	story

1. It looked like he was guilty, but then his lawyer presented some very compelling _____.
2. Everyone thinks she won the debate. She made a very compelling _____.
3. The movie tells a very compelling _____ about self-belief and determination.
4. He gave a compelling _____ of the causes and consequences of the disaster.
5. I don't see a compelling _____ why I should reject his offer.

COMMUNICATE

F Note an example next to each prompt below. Discuss with a partner.

1. a landmark near your home _____
2. something that brings headache relief _____
3. a place you visit because of its proximity _____
4. something you did on impulse _____

G What are the limitations of smartphone cameras today? Will smartphones of the future allow us to transcend these limitations? Why, or why not? Discuss with a partner.

> My smartphone camera isn't as customizable as an actual camera, but I think this will change …

UNIT 6

E F
G H

Viewing and Note-taking

LEARNING OBJECTIVES

- Watch and understand a talk about how phones can distract us
- Use the strong and weak forms of *that*

TEDTALKS

Erin Sullivan is a travel photographer with a passion for the outdoors. She is also a writer and the host of an online video series. In her TED Talk, *Does Photographing a Moment Steal the Experience from You?*, Sullivan explains how we probably take too many photos, and how we lose out because of this.

BEFORE VIEWING

A   Read the information about Erin Sullivan. Then discuss the questions below with a partner.

1. Sullivan begins her TED Talk by asking: "What is the most beautiful place you have ever been? And when you were there, did you take a picture of it?" How would you answer these questions?

2. Why do you think she chose to begin her TED Talk this way?

" Photography can be part of a beautiful experience. Just don't let it be a block between you and reality. "

WHILE VIEWING

B ▶ **LISTEN FOR MAIN IDEAS** Watch Segment 1 of Erin Sullivan's TED Talk. Check (✓) the ideas that she expresses.

1. ☐ It's pointless taking photos of places that have been photographed a lot.

2. ☐ Cameras help us notice details we might otherwise miss.

3. ☐ Photography can help us better appreciate the world and nature.

4. ☐ For photography to be enjoyable, we should avoid sharing our photos.

5. ☐ It's important that we take photographs for the right reasons.

C **INFER** What do you think Sullivan means by the following statement? Discuss with a partner.

"So this points to an important distinction: photography can enhance your experience if it's done intentionally. The intention piece is what matters."

D ▶ **LISTEN FOR DETAILS** Watch Segment 2 of Sullivan's TED Talk. Match the places to the experiences.

1. Alaska　　　_____　　_____

2. Tonga　　　_____　　_____

3. Uluru　　　_____　　_____

a. visited a sacred place　　　　**d.** her camera set up got in the way

b. photographed brown bears　　　**e.** had to take photos from far away

c. swam with whales　　　　　　**f.** shared a special experience with other photographers

E ▶ **LISTEN FOR PURPOSE** Match the photos (1–4) to the points Sullivan makes in her talk (a–d). Then watch the excerpts and check your answers.

1. _____ photo of Mesa Arch

2. _____ photo of Horseshoe Bend

3. _____ photo of bears

4. _____ photo of whales

a. Sometimes, taking photos enhances the experience.

b. Why take a photo if everyone else is taking the same photo?

c. People often take photos but miss out on the actual experience.

d. Sometimes, a camera can get in the way of an experience.

WORDS IN THE TALK
ultimately (adv) in the end
sacred (adj) important for religious reasons
intentionality (n) doing something for a specific, conscious reason
irreplaceable (adj) cannot be replaced

AFTER VIEWING

F **EVALUATE** Work with a partner. Read the four reasons why people often take photos (a–d). Match each reason to the category that best fits. Then think of your own reasons and add them to the chart.

a. to prove they were there

c. to appreciate the beauty of a place

b. as a way to bond

d. to capture a meaningful moment

Popular attractions	Special occasions
Scenic locations	Family and friends

G **APPLY** Think about the four types of photos in Exercise F. When would it be better to take fewer photos and be more involved in the experience instead?

PRONUNCIATION *Strong and weak forms of* that

H 🎧 Read the sentences from the TED Talk. What form of *that* should you use? Write **S** (strong) or **W** (weak). Listen and check.

> "Being eye to eye with these bears gave me a feeling of connection [1] **that** transcends words, and having my camera with me in this case enhanced [2] **that**."
>
> "[3] **That** group and I will have [4] **that** experience together and these images to look back on time and time again, and photography is what enabled us to share this in the first place."

Pronunciation Skill

Strong and Weak Forms of *That*

The word *that* has two forms. When it's used as a demonstrative to refer to something specific, we use the strong form, /ðæt/. When we use it to introduce a new clause in a sentence (e.g., the house that Jack built), we use the weak form, /ðət/.

1. _____   **2.** _____   **3.** _____   **4.** _____

I Write sentences containing the strong and weak forms of *that*. Then take turns reading your sentences aloud with a partner.

1. Strong: _____

2. Strong: _____

3. Weak: _____

4. Weak: _____

Thinking Critically

ANALYZE INFORMATION

A Look at the infographic. How superficial or meaningful would you consider each reason? Write the sentence numbers on the scale below. Discuss your ideas with a partner.

◄─────────────────────────────────────►

superficial   **meaningful**

B Work with a partner. Discuss the questions below.

1. Which two reasons relate most to what Erin Sullivan talked about in her TED Talk?
2. How did you rate these two reasons in Exercise A?
3. How popular do you think these two reasons for traveling are?

1 They want to take part in local cultural activities.

2 They want to taste some of the local food and drinks.

3 They want to shop or buy things from different countries.

4 They see travel as a means of personal development.

5 They want to visit places they saw on social media.

WHY DO YOUNG PEOPLE TRAVEL?

6 They want to post their travel photos on social media.

7 They want to experience something that's unique.

8 They want to make a positive difference in the places they visit.

9 They want to practice speaking the local language.

10 They want to learn about local cultures and traditions.

C 🎧 Listen to a talk about travel and take notes. Complete each sentence with a number.

1. Before the year _____, fewer than 800 people visited Trolltunga annually.

2. These days, about _____ people visit Trolltunga annually.

3. The number of visitors to Trolltunga has increased by more than _____%.

4. About _____ of young people visited places because they saw them on social media.

5. About _____ of young people say sharing vacation photos is important to them.

6. About _____ of young people would not go somewhere if they could not take photos.

COMMUNICATE   *Synthesize and evaluate ideas*

D Work with a partner. Read the conclusion of the talk in Exercise C. Then write a summary of the main idea of Sullivan's TED Talk. How are the focuses of the two talks similar? How are they different?

Conclusion of talk	Erin Sullivan's main idea
"It is perhaps unfortunate that so many young people are making travel decisions based on their phones. We shouldn't want to visit a destination simply because it's trending on social media. There is, after all, so much more to travel than just going to popular places that look good in photographs."	

E Read the four sentences below (a–d). To what extent do you agree with each idea? Write the letters on the scale. Then share your reasons with a partner. Discuss how you would change each idea so that you agree with it more.

⟵───────────────────────────────────⟶

strongly disagree   **strongly agree**

a. " … sometimes it seems like we are missing the point of going to [these places] … "

b. "The world needs every voice and perspective, and yours is included."

c. "Travel can be enriching, it can help us become better people, and it can teach us about the world and ourselves."

d. "It's perhaps unfortunate that so many young people are making travel decisions based on their phones."

> I strongly agree with sentence "a" because many people I know just want to collect stamps in their passports. They want to say they've visited a lot of countries, but …

> I disagree with "b." I'm not sure we need *every* voice, especially if many of the voices are all saying the same thing.

Putting It Together

ASSIGNMENT

Individual presentation: You are going to give a presentation on when taking photos and videos is worthwhile, and when it isn't.

PREPARE

A Review the unit. Consider all the ways people use their phones. In what ways can phones take away or lessen your enjoyment or appreciation of an experience?

_____

_____

_____

B Search your phone for three photos or videos that are meaningful to you, and that you think were worth taking. Then choose three that aren't really meaningful to you, and that you probably should not have bothered taking. Complete these steps.

1. Note down useful context, such as when and where the photos were taken.

2. Note down why each photo is or isn't meaningful.

3. Save the photos and videos to a folder that you can find again easily.

	Context	Why is it meaningful?
1.		
2.		
3.		

	Context	Why isn't it meaningful?
4.		
5.		
6.		

C Plan your presentation. Study your information in Exercise B. Come up with conclusions about when it's worthwhile to take photos and videos with your phone and when it isn't.

Photos and videos are worth taking when …	
Photos and videos are not worth taking when …	

D Look back at the vocabulary, pronunciation, and communication skills you've learned in this unit. What can you use in your presentation? Note any useful language below.

_____

_____

E Below are some questions to help you add context to your presentation. Use your answers to add to your notes in Exercise B.

- Who else was there?
- How were you feeling?
- What was the day like?
- What were you thinking of at the time?

> **Presentation Skill**
> **Providing Context**
>
> In her TED Talk, Erin Sullivan used photos to make certain points. She also provided context for each photo: she included useful or interesting information, such as where and when she took it, who she was with, and how she felt. Consider doing the same when presenting your own photos.

F Practice your presentation. Make use of the presentation skill that you've learned.

PRESENT

G Give your presentation to a partner. Watch their presentation and evaluate them using the Presentation Scoring Rubrics at the back of the book.

H Discuss your evaluation with your partner. Give feedback on two things they did well and two areas for improvement.

Checkpoint

Reflect on what you have learned. Check your progress.

I can … ☐ understand and use words to talk about phones and photography.

committed	compelling	impulse	landmark	limitation
proximity	solely	obligation	relief	transcend

☐ use collocations with the word *compelling*.

☐ watch and understand a talk about how phones can distract us from what matters.

☐ use the strong and weak forms of *that*.

☐ interpret an infographic about why young people travel.

☐ synthesize and evaluate ideas about phones, social media, and travel.

☐ provide context for photographs by including useful or interesting information.

☐ give a presentation on when taking photos and videos is worthwhile, and when it isn't.

Family members from different generations dance together to traditional music.

7

Generations

Q What are generations and do they matter?

In the photo, an older and younger family member dance together to traditional music, an example of different generations united in celebration. But in other situations older and younger people can feel separated by the generation they belong to. They may question–or criticize– the values and habits of people from other age brackets. But how much does age really matter? In this unit, we'll explore the idea of generational differences and to what extent the eras we grow up in shape who we are.

THINK and DISCUSS

1 Look at the photo and read the caption. How many different generations do you see?

2 Look at the essential question and the unit introduction. Think about your family, or people you know. Do you think people from different generations are very different?

Building Vocabulary

LEARNING OBJECTIVES

• Use ten words related to generations
• Use collocations with *debt*

LEARN KEY WORDS

A 🎧 Listen to and read the information below. What is the main idea?

    a. Some people have experienced easier lives than others.

    b. People from different generations are more alike than we think.

    c. The events that people live through affect their personalities.

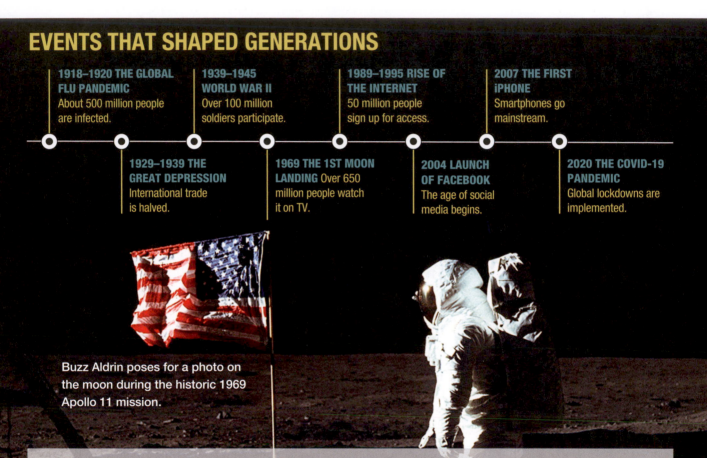

EVENTS THAT SHAPED GENERATIONS

1918–1920 THE GLOBAL FLU PANDEMIC
About 500 million people are infected.

1939–1945 WORLD WAR II
Over 100 million soldiers participate.

1989–1995 RISE OF THE INTERNET
50 million people sign up for access.

2007 THE FIRST iPHONE
Smartphones go mainstream.

1929–1939 THE GREAT DEPRESSION
International trade is halved.

1969 THE 1ST MOON LANDING Over 650 million people watch it on TV.

2004 LAUNCH OF FACEBOOK
The age of social media begins.

2020 THE COVID-19 PANDEMIC
Global lockdowns are implemented.

Buzz Aldrin poses for a photo on the moon during the historic 1969 Apollo 11 mission.

What makes us who we are? For many, the answer would be our DNA, or perhaps the people we grew up with. However, major events can also shape our personalities, to the extent that people born around the same time—who lived through the same events—often share similar **traits**.

Some of these major generation-shaping events can be positive. During the period of **optimism** after World War II, for instance, salaries rose, the cost of **housing** declined, and people had less **debt**. These favorable **circumstances** led to a baby boom and a new "baby boomer" generation that eventually developed a more positive **outlook** on life.

However, other generation-shaping events are more challenging. The global financial crash of 2008 and the COVID lockdowns of 2020, for example, impacted billions of young people negatively. They made it harder to find jobs and homes, and left many of the young people affected feeling anxious and **frustrated**.

It's easy to **misunderstand** people from different generations because they grew up in vastly different worlds. And that might explain why many are often so quick to form negative generational **stereotypes**. It's important though to consider the different social and financial **pressures** that made us all who we are.

B Look at the timeline in Exercise A. Discuss the questions below with a partner.

1. Which of the events do you think had the biggest influence on people's lives? Why?
2. How do you think the rest of the events would have affected people?
3. Which of the events have affected you personally? In what ways?
4. What other events do you think should be added? Why?

C Match the correct form of each word in **bold** from Exercise A with its meaning.

1. _____ circumstances
2. _____ debt
3. _____ frustrated
4. _____ housing
5. _____ misunderstand
6. _____ optimism
7. _____ outlook
8. _____ pressure
9. _____ stereotype
10. _____ trait

a. money a person must return or repay
b. the conditions or situation around a person or event
c. annoyed because you can't achieve what you want.
d. a simplistic generalization about a group
e. a characteristic or feature
f. something that makes life harder
g. to interpret incorrectly, or not as intended
h. different types of accommodation
i. a perspective on life and the future
j. the feeling that things will go well

D The words below collocate with the noun *debt*. Complete the sentences with the correct words.

pay off	run up	fall into	write off

1. The loan was issued decades ago, so the bank decided to _____ the debt.
2. He shops too much. He's going to _____ a huge debt on his credit card.
3. On her current salary, she won't be able to _____ her debt.
4. Things are fine now, but if I lose this contract, I'll definitely _____ debt.

E Complete the questions using the correct form of the words in **bold** from Exercise A.

1. What are some things that people often run up a _____ for?
2. What do people from other generations do that make you feel _____?
3. Does the cost of _____ in your town or city worry you?
4. When you think about the future, do you feel a sense of _____?
5. Why do people often feel offended by _____?
6. What are some _____ you admire in young people?

COMMUNICATE

F Work in a group. Discuss the questions in Exercise E. Give reasons and examples to support your opinions.

> I think college debt is quite common in this country.

> Yes, I agree. My cousin spends most of her salary paying off …

Viewing and Note-taking

LEARNING OBJECTIVES

- Watch an online discussion about issues affecting young people
- Match speakers with their ideas
- Recognize people's perspectives

BEFORE VIEWING

A Work in a group. Discuss the questions below.

1. On the whole, do you think life is harder now than it was a generation or two ago?
2. In what ways is life today easier?
3. In what ways is life today harder?

WHILE VIEWING

B ▶ **LISTEN FOR MAIN IDEAS** Watch Segment 1 of an online discussion. Choose the statement that best summarizes the purpose of the discussion.

a. to help a group of young people seek help for their problems

b. to find out the types of issues worrying young people these days

c. to allow people to express their opinions on different generations

C ▶ **MATCH SPEAKERS WITH IDEAS** Who matches the descriptions below? For each one, write **M** (Michael), **F** (Faye), or **C** (Carlos). Watch Segment 1 again to check your ideas.

1. _____ faces a lot of pressure to do well at school
2. _____ concerned about money and housing
3. _____ struggling to pay off his college debt
4. _____ says his grandmother thinks young people are lazy

> **Note-taking Skill**
>
> **Matching Speakers with Their Ideas**
>
> When you listen to more than one speaker, it helps to note down who says what. You don't have to write the person's name in full. Use abbreviations instead, like M1 for the first male speaker, or KJ if the speaker's name is Karla Jones.

D ▶ **LISTEN FOR DETAILS** Watch Segment 2 of the online discussion. Complete the notes below, using your own words when necessary.

> Mental health:
> - people are negatively affected by tech and social media
> - Carlos cut down [1]_____ and felt better
>
> Online privacy:
> - Faye used to post a lot on social media, but now doesn't
> - worries that the things we post [2]_____
> - believes that [3]_____ should do more
>
> Climate change:
> - [4]_____ thinks it's the biggest issue
> - weather & storms are worsening
> - [5]_____ don't seem to care
> - [6]_____ is optimistic: young people care
> - [7]_____ has a less positive outlook
> - [8]_____ says we can make a difference now

E ▶ **RECOGNIZE PERSPECTIVES** Watch some excerpts from the online discussion. Is the second person presenting a new perspective (**N**) or echoing the perspective of the speaker before them (**E**)?

1. Excerpt 1 _____
2. Excerpt 2 _____
3. Excerpt 3 _____
4. Excerpt 4 _____

Listening Skill

Recognizing Perspectives

When presenting a different perspective, people sometimes use phrases like "I somewhat agree" or "I get what you're saying." But listen carefully for what comes after. Phrases like these often help introduce differing viewpoints in a more polite way.

AFTER VIEWING

F **EVALUATE** A serious problem is an important one, while an urgent problem is one that needs to be addressed soon. Look at the five issues mentioned in the online discussion. Where do you think they belong on the diagram? Write the numbers.

| 1. cost of living | 2. pressure at school | 3. mental health |
| 4. online privacy | 5. climate change | |

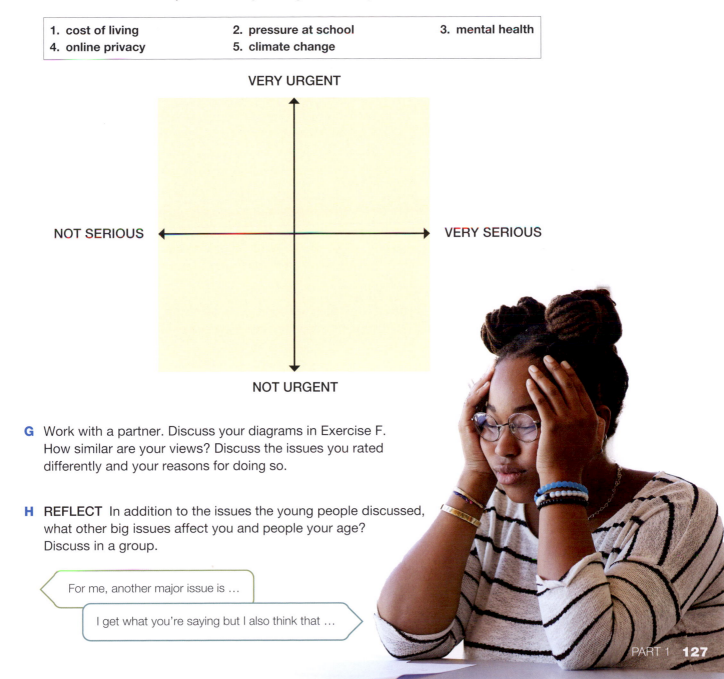

VERY URGENT

NOT SERIOUS ⟵——————⟶ VERY SERIOUS

NOT URGENT

G Work with a partner. Discuss your diagrams in Exercise F. How similar are your views? Discuss the issues you rated differently and your reasons for doing so.

H **REFLECT** In addition to the issues the young people discussed, what other big issues affect you and people your age? Discuss in a group.

For me, another major issue is …

I get what you're saying but I also think that …

Noticing Language

LISTEN FOR LANGUAGE   *Respond to other people's opinions*

A Work with a partner. Add the phrases from the box to the correct space in the chart.

I agree to some extent, but …	I'm with you.
Same here.	Good point.
I couldn't agree more.	I get what you're saying, but …
I wish I shared your …	I think you're missing the point.
Do you really think so?	That's so true.

> **Communication Skill**
>
> **Responding to Other People's Opinions**
>
> When somebody shares an opinion with you, you don't always have to fully agree or disagree with them. Partially agreeing or disagreeing with someone is useful when you want to present an alternative view while keeping the conversation friendly and polite.

Phrases that express agreement	Phrases that express disagreement

B Look at the phrases that express disagreement in Exercise A. Which ones do you feel are more direct? Which are more tactful? Discuss with a partner.

C 🎧 Listen to some excerpts from the online discussion in Lesson B. Complete the second speaker's responses. How strongly do you think each speaker agrees or disagrees? Discuss with a partner.

1. M: They think that we're lazy, and that we're anxious all the time.

   C: Yeah, _____. I certainly don't identify with those traits.

2. G: I'd say that in general, we both probably misunderstand each other.

   M: Hmm … _____.

3. G: I think the big social media companies should definitely do more to protect that.

   C: _____.

4. G: Plus, in twenty or so years, we'll be the ones in charge, and then we'll be able to do even more.

   C: _____ optimism, but I'm afraid my outlook isn't as positive.

COMMUNICATE

D Work with a partner. Complete these conversations in your own words. Then practice the conversations aloud. Take turns to be each speaker.

1. A: A lot of people worry about money, but in my view, our health is much more important.

   B: _____ .

2. A: _____ .

   B: I couldn't agree more. That's exactly how I feel, too!

3. A: _____ .

   B: I wish I shared your _____ .

4. A: Personally, I worry about work-life balance.

   B: _____ .

E Note your opinions about the topics below. Then work in a group and express your views. Agree or disagree with each other, but keep it polite and friendly.

Do you think …

1. a college or university degree is necessary to succeed in life?

2. working from home is better than working in an office?

3. children are exposed to technology too soon in life?

> I don't think that a college degree is really necessary.

> Do you really think so? Personally, …

Communicating Ideas

LEARNING OBJECTIVES

- Use appropriate language for responding to other people's opinions
- Collaborate to compare the concerns of people from different generations

---

ASSIGNMENT

Task: You are going to collaborate with a partner to compare the concerns of people from three different generations.

LISTEN FOR INFORMATION

A 🎧 **LISTEN FOR MAIN IDEAS** Listen to a conversation between two people and take notes. Then answer the questions.

1. What are the two people discussing?

   a. the problems and concerns they have in life

   b. how to solve a problem they're facing

2. How old are the two people in the conversation likely to be?

   a. They are probably in their 30s.

   b. They are probably in their 50s.

3. What is unique about many people close to that age?

   a. They have to worry about both health and financial problems.

   b. They have to worry about people from two other generations.

B 🎧 **LISTEN FOR DETAILS** Use your notes and complete the sentences below. Then think about who made each statement and circle **W** for woman or **M** for man. Listen again and check your answers.

1. These days, I _____ all the time, and
   I _____ longer, too.   W   M

2. Don't even get me started on _____.
   The _____ of everything is going up ....   W   M

3. The _____ is a mess, and the _____
   seems to get worse every time I turn on the news.   W   M

4. My mom's _____ again, but I'm afraid my dad
   needs a few more _____.   W   M

5. They can't find good _____, so they can't
   pay their _____ or their _____.   W   M

6. It's hard to be in the _____ and have to worry
   about _____ *and* _____.   W   M

C Work with a partner. Think about people you know who are in their 40s or 50s. Do they share any of the concerns that the speakers mentioned? Which ones?

COLLABORATE

D Work with a partner. Which groups would be most concerned about the items below? Write the letters (a–i) in the Venn diagram.

a. children   **d.** housing   **g.** grades

b. climate   **e.** career   **h.** parents

c. health   **f.** money   **i.** the attitudes of other generations

teenagers   people in their 30s

people in their 50s

E Work with another pair. Compare your Venn diagrams and explain your answers. Respond to each other's opinions and ask follow-up questions.

Checkpoint

Reflect on what you have learned. Check your progress.

I can ... understand and use words related to generations.

| circumstances | debt | frustrated | housing | misunderstand |
| optimism | outlook | pressure | stereotype | trait |

use collocations with *debt*.

watch and understand an online discussion about issues affecting young people.

match speakers with their ideas.

listen for and recognize people's perspectives.

notice language for responding to other people's opinions.

use language for agreeing or disagreeing with people's opinions politely.

collaborate and communicate effectively to compare the concerns of different generations.

An excited skydiver, thousands of feet above Ohau, in Hawaii, U.S.A.

Building Vocabulary

LEARNING OBJECTIVES

- Use ten words related to generational stereotypes
- Understand forms of *pragmatic* and *idealistic*

LEARN KEY WORDS

A 🎧 Listen to and read the passage below. How can stereotypes help us, and how can they harm us? Discuss with a partner.

> **Painting with a Broad Brush**
>
> How are people older and younger than you different? Are they stubborn and closed-minded, or independent and wise? Are they selfish and **entitled**, or tech-savvy and innovative? Now think about what you've just done. This sort of broad generalizing about people is stereotyping, and it's something we do all the time.
>
> Stereotyping is useful because it allows us to make sense of a complicated world. It helps us make quick predictions about people's **values**, traits, and actions. We spot patterns of behavior in groups of people and create mental shortcuts based on these patterns, which we then use to make interactions with new people easier.
>
> But while it's true that people from similar backgrounds often share similarities, it's easy to see how applying stereotypes broadly can cause problems. Millennials, for example, are often seen as **idealistic**. It would, however, be unfair to regard all millennials as unrealistically optimistic: obviously, many are **pragmatic** and capable of practical compromises.
>
> Because some stereotypes **radically** oversimplify reality, stereotyping is often seen as negative. Still, it's impossible—even impractical—to avoid stereotyping completely. Perhaps the **appropriate** thing to do is to simply be aware of our stereotypes and learn to treat people as distinct individuals.

B Work with a partner. Discuss the questions below.

1. Look at the photo and read the caption. What stereotype(s) does this person defy?

2. What other stereotypes do you know about? How true do you think they are?

C Match each word in **bold** from Exercise A with its meaning.

1. _____ believing that very good things can be achieved (even when unrealistic)

2. _____ correct or suitable for a specific time or situation

3. _____ realistic, practical, and sensible

4. _____ feeling like you deserve something you have not earned

5. _____ fundamentally, completely

6. _____ beliefs about what is right that affect how a person acts

D Read the excerpts from Leah Georges's TED Talk in Lesson F. Choose the options that best complete the definitions of the words in **bold**.

> " … in just the last several years, we've seen millennials **overtake** Generation X to be the most represented generation in the **workforce**."
>
> "This is a generation **characterized** by hard work. In fact, we can thank this generation for the term 'workaholic.'"
>
> " … we have to meet people in their only-ness, that is, that spot in the world where only we stand … But this requires **flexibility** and curiosity."

1. To **overtake** means to *become bigger than / get ahead of* someone else.

2. The **workforce** refers to all the *people who work / places to work* in a country.

3. If you're **characterized** by something, that thing *affects you negatively / describes you well*.

4. **Flexibility** is the ability to *adapt to situations / understand other people*.

E The adjectives *pragmatic* and *idealistic* are often thought of as opposites. Complete the sentences below using the words in the box.

pragmatic	pragmatist	pragmatism	idealistic	idealist	idealism

1. She's known for her attention to detail and her _____.

2. I'm not a(n) _____, but I think it's important for us to dream big.

3. We shouldn't get carried away. Our ideas need to be _____.

4. I lost my youthful _____ soon after I graduated and got a job.

5. He always sets realistic expectations. He's a bit of a(n) _____.

6. He thinks we should do more, but I think he's being too _____.

COMMUNICATE

F Note an example next to each prompt below. Discuss with a partner.

1. a situation you were in that required flexibility _____

2. someone you know who is idealistic _____

3. a situation in which it pays to be pragmatic _____

G Work with a partner. Read the statements below. Do you agree with them? Why, or why not?

1. Stereotypes usually characterize people in ways that are radically untrue.

2. It's idealistic to think that we can change people's negative stereotypes.

> Some stereotypes are radically untrue, but …

> I don't think it's idealistic to want to change negative stereotypes …

Viewing and Note-taking

LEARNING OBJECTIVES

- Watch and understand a talk about generational stereotyping
- Use stress in prepositional phrases

TEDTALKS

Leah Georges is a psychology professor and researcher. She is interested in understanding leadership and in using data to find solutions to the kinds of complex problems people face in the world today. In her TED Talk, *How Generational Stereotypes Hold Us Back at Work*, she suggests a way to help different generations interact more effectively at work.

BEFORE VIEWING

A Leah Georges begins her TED Talk by saying that "For the first time … in modern history, we have five generations interacting at work." Discuss the questions below with a partner.

1. How do you think this affects the modern workplace?

2. What (if anything) should businesses do to adapt?

> **❝** We are so much more similar than we are different, and we're hearing this consistently. **❞**

WHILE VIEWING

B ▶ **LISTEN FOR DETAILS** Watch Segment 1 of Leah Georges's TED Talk. Complete the chart with the information she gives about different generations.

• Born between [1]_____ and 1943 • Called the [2]_____ Generation, the matures, or the silents. • Known for being self-sacrificing	
• Born between 1944 and [3]_____ • Called boomers • Known for working hard and being "workaholics"	
• Born between [4]_____ and 1980 • Called Generation X, or the [5]_____ generation or the latchkey generation • Interested in work-life balance	
• Born between [6]_____ and the end of the century • Called [7]_____ • Known for being both pragmatic and idealistic	
• Born after the year [8]_____ • Called Generation Z • May still be studying or working as interns	

C ▶ **LISTEN FOR MAIN IDEAS** Watch Segment 1 again. Circle the main point Georges makes after describing the different generations at length. Why do you think she makes this point so late? Discuss with a partner.

a. Differences between the generations are a major issue for companies.

b. People can be divided into more generations than researchers thought.

c. Many companies aren't doing enough to attract younger workers.

d. Many of our assumptions about generational differences are wrong.

WORDS IN THE TALK

workaholic (n) a person who works too much and seems addicted to it
self-fulfilling prophecy (phr) when the belief that something is certain causes people to actually make it happen
navigate (v) to find a way to manage a difficult situation
aloof (adj) unfriendly and unwilling to engage with others

D ▶ **INFER** Watch Segment 2 of Georges's TED Talk. Check (✓) the statements that you think she's likely to agree with.

1. ☐ People across different generations want similar things at work.

2. ☐ Managers need to be more aware of key generational differences.

3. ☐ Managers are better off adopting a more individualized approach.

4. ☐ An individualized management approach requires less flexibility.

E ▶ **LISTEN FOR EXAMPLES** Watch Segment 2 again. For each problem (1–3), write the generation Georges talks about. Then match the underlying reasons (a–c) with the three problems.

1. Angry all the time _____

2. Aloof at work _____

3. Asks for a raise _____

a. _____ burdened by heavy debt

b. _____ anxious about not having a job soon

c. _____ exhausted from caring for the family

AFTER VIEWING

F **REFLECT** In her talk, Georges suggests we treat people as individuals rather than as members of a generation. Discuss the questions below in a group.

1. What are some stereotypes people from other generations have of your generation?

2. Are you treated more often as an individual or as a member of your generation by people outside your generation?

> People outside my generation often think we're resourceful and innovative …

> I think people outside my generation usually treat me as an individual. My lecturers, for example …

PRONUNCIATION   *Stress in prepositional phrases*

G 🎧 Listen to Leah Georges say the phrases below. Underline the words she stresses. What happens to the preposition?

1. the wheels on the bus

2. a little aloof at work

3. asks for a raise

H Work with a partner. Look back at the passage in Lesson E and find examples of sentences that include a prepositional phrase. Underline the stressed words, mark where words run together, and consider if the pronunciation of the preposition is reduced. Practice reading the sentences aloud to each other.

Pronunciation Skill

Stress in Prepositional Phrases

Prepositional phrases consist of a preposition (e.g., *on*, *at*, etc.) followed by a noun. Usually, the main content word just before the preposition is stressed, and the noun inside the prepositional phrase. The preposition itself is only weakly pronounced, so its sound is often reduced, or may run together (link) with other words.

LEARNING OBJECTIVES

- Interpret an infographic about what workers want
- Synthesize and evaluate ideas about different generations in the workplace

ANALYZE INFORMATION

A Look at the infographic and answer the questions. Discuss your answers with a partner.

1. What do you think is the difference between regular and continuous feedback?

2. What are some ways to make a workplace more informal?

3. What can companies do to be more diverse and inclusive?

4. How can companies offer employees a good work-life balance?

5. Which of the items listed is most important to you? Why?

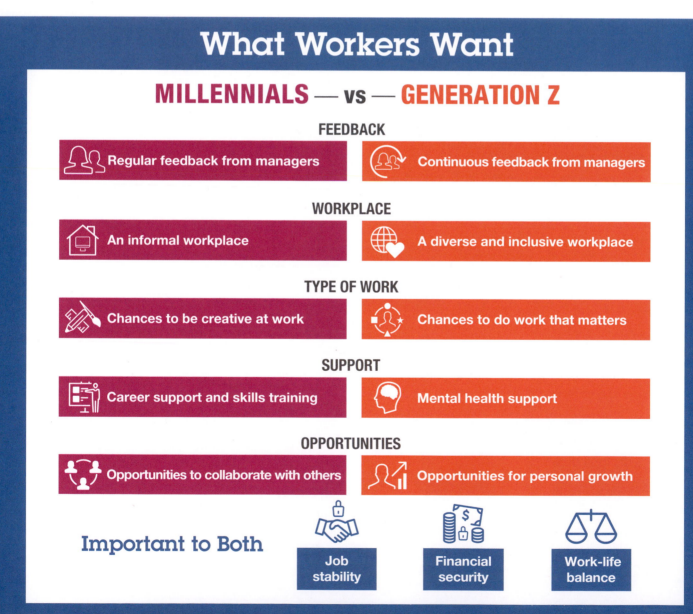

What Workers Want

MILLENNIALS — vs — GENERATION Z

FEEDBACK

| Regular feedback from managers | Continuous feedback from managers |

WORKPLACE

| An informal workplace | A diverse and inclusive workplace |

TYPE OF WORK

| Chances to be creative at work | Chances to do work that matters |

SUPPORT

| Career support and skills training | Mental health support |

OPPORTUNITIES

| Opportunities to collaborate with others | Opportunities for personal growth |

Important to Both

| Job stability | Financial security | Work-life balance |

B 🎧 Listen to a talk about different generations in the workforce. Check (✓) the correct answers. More than one answer may be possible.

1. According to the speaker, how have offices changed?

    a. ☐ Technology has changed the way people work.

    b. ☐ Offices have become more crowded.

    c. ☐ Open office layouts have become more common.

2. What can we infer about generations in the workforce today?

    a. ☐ Millennial employees outnumber Gen X employees.

    b. ☐ There are more Gen Z workers than Gen X workers.

    c. ☐ Gen Z workers will become more common.

3. What are some ways companies can adapt to different generations?

    a. ☐ Make workplaces and dress codes less formal.

    b. ☐ Use different management styles.

    c. ☐ Create cross-generational mentoring programs.

C Work in a group. Discuss the questions below. Give reasons to support your opinions.

1. The speaker in Exercise B encourages companies to adapt to the changing workforce. Do you think it's worth a company's time and resources to do this?

2. Is a company more or less likely to succeed if it doesn't adapt to younger workers, but instead expects its younger employees to adapt to the company?

3. The speaker also talks about younger and older employees mentoring each other. How useful do you think such a mentoring program would be?

4. As a young employee, what could you learn from such a program?

COMMUNICATE   *Synthesize and evaluate ideas*

D Think about the points made in Leah Georges's TED Talk and the ones in this lesson. Discuss with a partner.

1. How similar or different are Leah Georges's views on intergenerational workplaces from those described in this lesson?

2. Which points would Leah Georges probably disagree with, and why?

3. Which do you agree with more: Leah Georges's perspective, or the points made in this lesson?

E How do you think Georges would probably respond to each statement below? Work with a partner and write the responses she might give. Then discuss with another pair.

1. In general, people of different generations have very different working styles.

2. Companies should adapt to individual workers, not to generations of workers.

3. Generations definitely exist, though not everybody identifies strongly with their generation.

4. Everyone has something to offer at work, no matter how old or young they are.

Putting It Together

ASSIGNMENT

Group presentation: Your group is going to give a presentation on the ideal workplace for people of your generation.

PREPARE

A Review the unit. Answer these questions about two generations: your generation and one other generation. Discuss your answers with a partner.

1. What are people from these two generations called?
2. What key events have shaped these two generations?
3. What traits are often associated with these two generations?
4. What things do people of these two generations often want?

B Work with your group. Search online for "best companies to work for." Choose one company each and research reasons why it is considered a great place to work. Make notes.

_____

_____

_____

_____

C Plan your presentation. Compare your notes from Exercise B and discuss the top three things you would like your ideal workplace to have. Add them to the chart below and make notes about each one.

Things I would like in my ideal workplace	Why it's good for people of my generation	How people from other generations might feel about it

D Look back at the vocabulary, pronunciation, and communication skills you've learned in this unit. What can you use in your presentation? Note any useful language below.

_____

_____

_____

_____

E Below are some Dos and Don'ts to help you deliver a dynamic presentation. Think about how you can make use of these ideas your talk.

DO	DON'T
Use hand gestures.	Apologize. (*sorry*, *I'm nervous*)
Walk around.	Use fillers. (*um*, *uh*, *ah*, etc.)
Make eye contact.	Whisper.
Emphasize key points.	Speak in a monotone.

> **Presentation Skill**
> **Delivering a Dynamic Presentation**
>
> In her TED Talk, Leah Georges clearly attempts to make eye contact with audience members in different parts of the room. She also moves around and uses her hands to avoid seeming static. Dynamic presenters are often more engaging, so consider using techniques like these when you present.

F Practice your presentation. Make use of the presentation skill that you've learned.

PRESENT

G Give your presentation to another group. Watch their presentation and evaluate them using the Presentation Scoring Rubrics at the back of the book.

H Discuss your evaluation with the other group. Give feedback on two things they did well and two areas for improvement.

Checkpoint

Reflect on what you have learned. Check your progress.

I can ... ☐ understand and use words related to generational stereotypes.

appropriate	**characterize**	**entitled**	**flexibility**	**idealistic**
overtake	**pragmatic**	**radically**	**values**	**workforce**

☐ use forms of *pragmatic* and *idealistic*.

☐ watch and understand a talk about generational stereotyping.

☐ use stress in prepositional phrases.

☐ interpret an infographic about what young people want at work.

☐ synthesize and evaluate ideas about different generations in the workplace.

☐ deliver a dynamic presentation.

☐ give a presentation on the ideal workplace for my generation.

Brazilian dancers perform in a carnival parade in London, U.K.

8

Mixing Cultures

Q Is cultural exchange always a good thing?

In the photo, Brazilian dancers fill Queen Elizabeth Olympic Park in London, U.K., with color and movement as spectators from around the world look on. In this example of cultural exchange, the dancers are clearly happy for people from other cultural backgrounds to participate in the experience. But are people always eager to share aspects of their culture with outsiders? In this unit, we'll explore the topic of cultural exchange, and consider whether it's possible for it to go too far.

THINK and DISCUSS

1 Look at the photo and read the caption. Do you have celebrations like this where you are from? How are they similar? How are they different?

2 Look at the essential question and the unit introduction. Can you think of cultural practices or traditions that people might not want to share with outsiders?

Building Vocabulary

LEARNING OBJECTIVES

- Use ten words related to cultural appreciation and appropriation
- Use collocations with *consideration, disrespect, offend,* and *rejection*

LEARN KEY WORDS

A Listen to and read the information below. Discuss the questions with a partner and give reasons to support your opinions.

1. Does the information present an overall positive, negative, or neutral view of globalization?

2. What does the passage suggest we all try to do, regardless of how we feel about globalization?

THE ROAD TO GLOBALIZATION

Since ancient times, trade and the movement of people have led to the exchange of goods, ideas, and beliefs among societies. Today, thanks to improvements in technology, these exchanges are happening much more frequently. Something that **originates** in one country can now spread quickly and easily to other regions.

This phenomenon—known as **globalization**—is a **controversial** topic. Some people worry about its effect on small, local businesses, or how new cultural influences could change their society in ways that feel non-traditional or **inappropriate**.

But despite this sometimes understandable resistance, there's no doubt that globalization brings many benefits, too. Businesses enjoy increased trade; cities become exciting and multicultural; and people get to enjoy the best food, art, and entertainment the world has to offer.

Whatever one's feelings are about globalization, one thing remains true: it's not going away. It therefore makes sense for us to be open and sensitive to other cultures: to not **disrespect** foreign traditions, or **label** them as strange; and to replace the **rejection** of different cultural practices with **genuine** appreciation. At the very least, we could try not to **offend** each other and show some **consideration** instead.

THE ROAD TO GLOBALIZATION

7TH TO 15TH CENTURY *The Silk Road*
Luxury goods like spices and silk were traded by sea and land from the east to the west.

15TH TO 18TH CENTURY *Age of Discovery*
Advances in science and shipping helped European nations create new routes to trade raw materials.

19TH TO MID-20TH CENTURY *The Industrial Age*
The industrial revolution allowed goods to be created quickly and cheaply, and traded around the world.

1950s TO 2008 *Pre-modern Globalization*
The development of global supply chains and computer technology made global trade easier and more profitable.

2009 TO THE PRESENT *The Modern World*
Improvements in technology lead to digital goods and services that can be traded more easily than physical ones.

B Match the correct form of each word in **bold** from Exercise A with its meaning.

1. _____ causing a lot of heated disagreement and discussion

2. _____ not suitable or acceptable

3. _____ sincere, real, true

4. _____ to show a lack of appropriate courtesy or appreciation

5. _____ refusal to accept or be open to something

6. _____ increasing connections, interdependence and similarity between countries

7. _____ regard for the feelings and concerns of others

8. _____ to come from a specific place or time

9. _____ to use a specific word or phrase to describe something, often unfairly

10. _____ to do or say something that upsets people

C Complete the collocations below using the correct words in **bold** from Exercise A.

1. risk/fear _____

2. take care not to _____ someone

3. show _____ for others

4. treat someone with _____

D Complete the passage using the words in the box. One word is extra.

consideration	offend	controversial	genuine	inappropriate

Cultural differences can exist in areas you don't expect. For example, some of the gestures you use could be considered ¹_____ in other cultures. Topics you think are neutral could be considered ²_____. And jokes you think are safe could cause ³_____ anger. Be culturally sensitive when interacting with others: your ⁴_____ will go a long way.

COMMUNICATE

E Work in a group. Discuss the questions below.

1. What are some cultural objects, trends, or practices that have spread quickly from one country to other parts of the world?

2. Do you agree that globalization is not going away? Why, or why not?

> I think globalization is here to stay. It's impossible to avoid because …

Viewing and Note-taking

LEARNING OBJECTIVES

- Watch a lecture about cultural appropriation
- Practice visual note-taking
- Distinguish facts from opinions

BEFORE VIEWING

A 🎧 Listen to a person talking about a concert performance she saw online. Then complete the notes below.

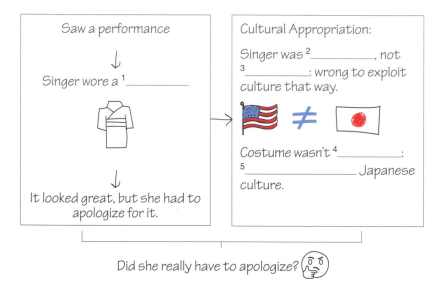

> Saw a performance
> ↓
> Singer wore a ¹_____
>
> It looked great, but she had to apologize for it.

> Cultural Appropriation:
>
> Singer was ²_____, not ³_____: wrong to exploit culture that way.
>
> 🇺🇸 ≠ 🇯🇵
>
> Costume wasn't ⁴_____: ⁵_____ Japanese culture.

Did she really have to apologize?

Note-taking Skill

Practicing Visual Note-taking

Visual note-taking is a way of combining written notes with visual elements, including simple illustrations, boxes, lines, colors, shapes and symbols. The visuals can be added while listening or after. Studies show that visual note-taking can help people concentrate better and remember more content.

WHILE VIEWING

B ▶ **LISTEN FOR MAIN IDEAS** Watch a lecture about cultural appropriation and **take notes**. Then circle the statement below that best describes the main purpose of the lecture.

a. to show how we are all guilty of cultural appropriation

b. to explain that cultural appropriation is not a real issue

c. to explain why we shouldn't wear clothes from other cultures

d. to show that cultural appropriation is a complex and nuanced issue

C ▶ **PRACTICE VISUAL NOTE-TAKING** Read the Note-taking Skill box and look at the notes in Exercise A. What visual elements do you see? Listen again to the lecture and add your own visuals to the notes you took earlier. Then show a partner. Do you think visual note-taking is useful for you?

D ▶ **LISTEN FOR FACTS AND OPINIONS** Read the statements below. Then watch some excerpts from the lecture. Are the statements below facts (**F**) or opinions (**O**)?

1. The people were exploiting other people's cultures.   **F   O**

2. Regular people can be accused of cultural appropriation. **F   O**

3. The speaker was guilty of cultural appropriation.   **F   O**

4. Appropriation is too strong a term when there's genuine appreciation.   **F   O**

Listening Skill

Distinguishing Facts from Opinions

Speakers do not always use statistics or mention research when giving facts. Similarly, they do not always introduce opinions with phrases like *In my view*. To distinguish fact from opinion, try listening for evidence, or ask yourself if there are other commonly-held, plausible perspectives.

E ▶ **LISTEN FOR DETAILS** The lecture describes how cultural items and practices often migrate from region to region. Match the steps of this process (a–d) to their definitions (1–4). Watch the excerpt from the lecture and check your answers.

a. _____ cultural adoption

b. _____ cultural appreciation

c. _____ cultural assimilation

d. _____ cultural adaptation

1. modify something to suit one's own culture

2. fully accept something as part of one's own culture

3. admire something from a different culture

4. take or use something from a different culture

F ▶ **SEQUENCE** Number the four steps from Exercise E in the correct order. Watch the excerpt again and check your answers.

a. _____ cultural adoption

b. _____ cultural appreciation

c. _____ cultural assimilation

d. _____ cultural adaptation

AFTER VIEWING

G **REFLECT** Work in a group. Discuss the questions below.

1. Do you know of any instances when people were accused of cultural appropriation? Do you think the accusation was justified?

2. Upon reflection, have you ever done anything that could be viewed as cultural appropriation by some?

> Hip hop culture isn't really part of my own culture, but I'm not sure if wearing hip hop fashion counts as cultural appropriation …

Women dressed in traditional yukata participate in a local "street cooling" festival in Tokyo, Japan.

Noticing Language

LISTEN FOR LANGUAGE *Choose the right voice*

A Read the excerpts from the lecture in Lesson B. Underline any verbs that are in the passive voice.

1. " … here are two examples of what cultural appropriation could look like."

2. "Here, we have someone wearing a costume that's loosely inspired by Native American culture."

3. " … jazz is from the U.S.A., but it was heavily influenced by African musical traditions and cultures."

4. "Some things we associate with one culture actually originated from a different culture."

5. "But if this is done purely for financial gain, that's a red flag."

> **Communication Skill**
> **Choosing the Right Voice**
>
> The active voice focuses on the person or thing "doing" the action. Active sentences tend to be clear and direct. The passive voice takes away this focus on the person or thing doing the action. This is often useful, for example, when it's more important to focus on the person or thing *affected* by the action, when we don't know who did the action, or when we'd prefer not to assign blame.

B 🎧 Complete the sentences using the verbs in parentheses and the correct voice. Then listen to the excerpts from the lecture and check your answers.

1. "And in this picture, the person has a hairstyle that _____ (*associate*) closely with Black culture."

2. "We had an amazing time, but it was hot and humid, and we _____ (*not pack*) suitable clothes."

3. "And if it _____ (*not do*) with respect or consideration for the other culture, then that's probably as clear-cut as cultural appropriation gets."

Brazilians practicing the martial art capoeira.

C Read the sentences below. Circle the voice that you think is more appropriate. Compare your answers with a partner and discuss the reasons for your answers.

1. **a.** It was put together rather quickly, so mistakes were unavoidable.
   b. He put it together rather quickly, so mistakes were unavoidable.
2. **a.** People in China invented fireworks more than a thousand years ago.
   b. Fireworks were invented in China more than a thousand years ago.
3. **a.** He helps many people every week at the nursing home.
   b. Many people are helped by him every week at the nursing home.
4. **a.** His work was overlooked while he was alive, but it's celebrated now.
   b. People overlooked his work while he was alive, but they celebrate it now.

D 🎧 Work with a partner. Complete the passage using the correct form of each verb in parentheses. Then listen to check your answers.

The English language ¹_____ (*know*) to have many more words than most other

languages. But why is this so? The reason is largely due to cultural assimilation. As a result

of foreign invasions and centuries of international trade, words from many other languages

²_____ (*pick up*) by English speakers. Early English ³_____

(*influence*) mostly by Latin and French, but also by ancient Greek and various Germanic languages.

Later, when advances in ship-building ⁴_____ (*make*) it possible for British traders to

⁵_____ (*visit*) regions like Asia, North and South America, and Africa, words from

even more languages ⁶_____ (*add*) to English. Today, this process continues. It has

even ⁷_____ (*speed up*) by the internet and other communication technologies.

COMMUNICATE

E The words in the box describe different aspects of culture. Choose two aspects and think of an example for each. They can be from any culture. Write clues for each of your examples.

food and drink	art	books	dance	design	architecture
movies and TV	games	clothes	music	sports	special days

- Capoeira: This is a type of martial art from Brazil. It is practiced by …
- Sari: This is a type of clothing worn by women in India. It is often worn during special occasions …

F Work in a group. Take turns reading your clues from Exercise E to each other, but don't reveal what you're describing. Your group has to guess, and ask follow-up questions if they are not sure.

> It's a type of martial art from Brazil. It's practiced by both dancers and martial artists …

> Is it capoeira?

Communicating Ideas

ASSIGNMENT

Task: You are going to collaborate in a group to analyze some cultural items or practices that have influenced other cultures or been influenced by them.

LISTEN FOR INFORMATION

A 🎧 **LISTEN FOR MAIN IDEAS** Listen to the beginning of a talk about Italian food. What is the main idea of the talk? Circle the correct answer.

a. how American culture has influenced Italian food

b. how Italian food has influenced food in the United States

c. how popular Italian food is around the world

B 🎧 **LISTEN FOR DETAILS** Listen to the entire talk. Check (✓) the points that the speaker makes.

1. ☐ Foods like garlic bread and pepperoni pizza are not from Italy.

2. ☐ When Italians moved to the United States, they adapted traditional recipes.

3. ☐ Traditional Italian cooking uses a lot of butter and cheese.

4. ☐ Olive oil and fresh vegetables were cheaper in the United States than in Italy.

5. ☐ American entertainment has influenced people from many countries.

6. ☐ Italian-American dishes seldom appear on TV shows and movies.

7. ☐ Visitors to Italy can order Italian-American dishes in some tourist places.

8. ☐ In the modern world, it is common for cultures to influence each other.

C Work in a group. Discuss the questions below. Support your ideas with reasons, details, and examples.

1. Did the speaker say anything that surprised you?

2. The speaker says that cultures changing and shaping each other is neither good nor bad: it's simply a reality of life. How much do you agree, and why?

3. Which three cultures have had the biggest influence on your own culture?

> I'm surprised that so many dishes I thought were Italian aren't actually Italian!

> I think cultural exchange is a good thing. It's exciting, and we all benefit by learning from each other.

COLLABORATE

D Work with a partner. Think of two cultural items or practices: one that has influenced another culture, and one that has been influenced by another culture. Use the categories in Lesson C, Exercise E to help you. Complete the chart below.

Country or region	
Item or practice	
Culture that influenced it	

Country or region	
Item or practice	
Culture that has been influenced by it	

E Work with another pair. Share your charts from Exercise D. Ask each other questions to learn more about these cultural items and practices. How do you think people from the influencing cultures feel about the things you listed?

> I think I'd feel proud if I knew my culture had such a strong influence on another culture ...

> I'm not sure I'd appreciate another culture changing something I feel is so culturally important to me ...

Checkpoint

Reflect on what you have learned. Check your progress.

I can ... understand and use words related to cultural appreciation and appropriation.

consideration	**controversial**	**disrespect**	**genuine**	**globalization**
inappropriate	**label**	**offend**	**originate**	**rejection**

use collocations with *consideration*, *disrespect*, *offend*, and *rejection*.

watch and understand a lecture about cultural appropriation.

take notes with visuals.

distinguish facts and opinions.

notice the use of the active and passive voice.

use the active and passive voice to talk about cultural influences.

collaborate and communicate effectively to analyze different cultural influences.

Benin Bronzes displayed at the British Museum in London, U.K.

Building Vocabulary

LEARNING OBJECTIVES

- Use ten words to talk about culturally important objects
- Use forms of *acquire*, *campaign*, *discrimination*, *feature*, and *initiative*

LEARN KEY WORDS

A  Listen to and read the passage below. How do museums acquire artifacts? Why might some museum items be controversial? Discuss with a partner.

Missing Pieces

Museums play an important role in communities and countries around the world. By preserving items of historical and cultural significance, museums make the history and culture of these places more **accessible**. They also educate visitors and help locals develop a deeper sense of their own cultural identity and their country's **rich** history.

To remain popular, museums need to feature exhibits of value and importance. These can be obtained in a number of ways. Some objects, for instance, are received as gifts or purchased from their rightful owners. In other cases, museums **acquire** their **artifacts** through exchanges with other institutions. Museums might even excavate—or dig up—historically important sites or conduct fieldwork out in the natural world.

However, some museums house objects that were improperly acquired. These objects might have been purchased from someone other than their legal owner, or simply stolen. In such cases, people often want these objects returned. For instance, millions believe that the Benin Bronzes—displayed in museums across Europe and the United States—should be sent back to Nigeria. In fact, the Nigerian government has **campaigned** for decades for the **restitution** of these culturally significant objects. So far, only some of their appeals have been successful.

B Work with a partner. Discuss the questions below.

1. Different museums house different types of artifacts. How many types of museums can you think of? Which do you think are most culturally important?

2. Look at the photo. It shows art taken from Benin City in Nigeria over 100 years ago. Why might the Nigerian Government want these items back?

C Match the correct form of each word in **bold** from Exercise A with its meaning.

1. _____ to obtain or buy something

2. _____ an object of historical or cultural value

3. _____ the return of objects that were unfairly taken or stolen

4. _____ interesting because it is long and varied

5. _____ easy to obtain, reach, or understand

6. _____ to organize and push for political, social or systemic change

D Read the excerpts from Jim Chuchu's TED Talk in Lesson F. Choose the options that are closest to the meanings of the words in **bold**.

1. "If you live in New York or London, ... it's likely that you've visited an art museum that **features** a collection of African art."

   a. sells   **b.** displays

2. " ... 90% of sub-Saharan Africa's material cultural legacy is **housed** outside the African continent."

   a. stored   **b.** protected

3. "The more difficult part for us Kenyans was having to read through ... records from a time in history when Africans were on the receiving end of colonial force, violence, and **discrimination**."

   a. the unfair treatment of certain groups of people
   b. the unfair treatment and payment of workers

4. "We're not the only **initiative** of our kind. Across Africa and Asia, there are other projects asking similar questions about their cultural heritage."

   a. a decision or choice   **b.** a plan or movement

E Complete the chart below with the correct words. Then complete the sentences using the most suitable words.

Verb form	Noun form
campaign	
feature	
acquire	
	discrimination
	initiative

1. We shouldn't _____ against people who are different from us.

2. They launched a _____ to increase recycling in their community.

3. The phone was expensive, but he was pleased with his _____.

COMMUNICATE

F Work in a group. What museums have you visited, and what type of artifacts were housed there? Did the museum(s) feature just local artifacts, or artifacts from around the world?

> The museum I went to housed mainly local artifacts, but they also had …

Viewing and Note-taking

LEARNING OBJECTIVES

- Watch and understand a talk about cultural restitution
- Use emphasis

TEDTALKS

Jim Chuchu is a film director, photographer, musician, and visual artist. He was one of the founders of The Nest Collective, a group that promotes music, fashion, and art. In his TED Talk, *Why Are Stolen African Artifacts Still in Western Museums?*, he argues for the restitution of important cultural objects.

BEFORE VIEWING

A   Read the information about Jim Chuchu. Then work with a group and discuss the questions below.

1. Are there any objects you feel are significant to your culture?
2. Why do you think some people enjoy looking at cultural objects in museums?
3. Chuchu says cultural objects "help us remember who we are." What do you think he means by this?

" There can be no collective identity without collective memory, so we're asking for our objects to help us remember who we are. "

B ▶ **LISTEN FOR MAIN IDEAS** Watch Jim Chuchu's TED Talk. Check (✓) the set of notes below that better summarizes the main points of his talk.

☐ **Option 1:**

- Collections of African art can be found in cities around the world.

- Some of these objects are valuable, and some are not.

- People in Africa want these artifacts returned to their countries of origin.

- Some museums are returning them, but many objects are still lost or missing

☐ **Option 2:**

- Most African historical artifacts are housed in museums outside Africa.

- Some were acquired fairly, but many were stolen or misappropriated.

- The loss of these objects equates to a loss of culture.

- Many people are campaigning for the return of these ill-gotten artifacts.

C ▶ **LISTEN FOR DETAILS** Watch Chuchu's TED Talk again. Choose the best answer to complete each statement.

1. Chuchu gives New York and London as examples of cities that _____.

   a. are famous for their culture

   b. get a lot of visitors every year

2. The 2018 report claims that _____.

   a. almost all of Africa's art has been returned to Africa

   b. almost all of Africa's art is housed outside of Africa

3. According to Chuchu, a society without cultural objects _____.

   a. feels that other cultures are richer than their own

   b. fights more passionately to defend its culture

4. Chuchu lists burgers and pasta as examples of foods that _____.

   a. symbolize the erosion of Kenyan culture

   b. are generally disliked by people in Kenya

5. Chuchu's coalition has collected data about 32,000 _____.

   a. museums in Europe and North America with African art

   b. objects from Africa in museum collections outside Africa

---

WORDS IN THE TALK

confiscate (v) to take something away from somebody
sub-Saharan Africa (phr) African countries that lie south of the Sahara desert
public sphere (phr) the collective thoughts and conversations of a society
improperly (adv) dishonestly or not legally

AFTER VIEWING

D **EVALUATE** Read the opinions below (a–e) about cultural restitution. How much do you agree with them? Write the letters on the scale below. Then share your scale with a partner. Give reasons for your choices.

a. Art that was taken or stolen should be returned.

b. Art that was given or bought should **not** be returned.

c. Museums should return art to the country it's from, but only temporarily.

d. Museums have the right to keep foreign artifacts that they've taken care of for years.

e. Museums should have to pay fines for housing improperly acquired artifacts.

←————————————————————————————————→

strongly disagree   **strongly agree**

PRONUNCIATION *Use emphasis*

E 🎧 Listen to an excerpt from the TED Talk. Write the missing emphasized words below. Why do you think Chuchu emphasizes these words?

> "I'm an artist, and I tell stories for a living. To tell stories, you need imagination [1]_____ memory. And in Kenya, we have a [2]_____ in our memory. So much of what happened between the late 1800s until our independence in 1963 is missing because [3]_____ of the objects that tell our stories from that period are gone. According to a 2018 report on African cultural heritage, [4]_____ of sub-Saharan Africa's material cultural legacy is housed [5]_____ the African continent."

> **Pronunciation Skill**
> **Using Emphasis**
>
> It's normal to stress certain words in spoken English. However, speakers sometimes use additional stress to emphasize key points. This isn't the same as normal word stress, which is more consistent and predictable. Emphasis is more strongly pronounced and easily heard.

F 🎧 Read the sentences. Underline the words you think should be emphasized in order to make each sentence more impactful. Then listen. Did the speaker emphasize the words you chose?

1. It's never too late to make a difference.

2. The item was bought, but not from its rightful owner.

3. You're not giving the item to us. You're giving the item back to us.

4. Museums in Africa shouldn't have to prove that an item belongs to them. It's up to the museums in Europe to prove that the artifacts they house rightfully belong to them.

G Work with a partner. Take turns reading the sentences in Exercise F aloud. Remember to emphasize the correct words.

Thinking Critically

LEARNING OBJECTIVES

- Interpret an infographic about culturally significant objects
- Synthesize and evaluate ideas about cultural restitution

ANALYZE INFORMATION

A Look at the infographic and write short notes that summarize what it shows. Share your ideas with a partner.

_____

_____

WHERE ARE THEY?

- - - **DASHED LINE:** items are not housed in their home countries

—— **SOLID LINE:** items have been returned to their home countries

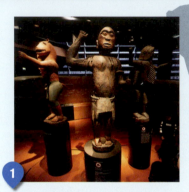

1
- Royal statues of the Kingdom of Dahomey
- Believed to have been taken by France between 1892 and 1894
- Returned to Benin by the *Musée du Quai Branly – Jacques Chirac* in 2021

2
- Cotton "Ghost Shirt" from the Native American Lakota people
- Housed in the Kelvingrove Museum in Glasgow, U.K. from 1892
- Returned to South Dakota, U.S.A., in 1999

3
- A stone moai statue from Rapa Nui (also called Easter Island)
- Housed in the National History Museum in Santiago, Chile, from 1870
- Returned to Rapa Nui in 2022

4
- Painted stone bust of Nefertiti, a queen of Egypt
- Housed in Germany since 1913
- Currently in the Neues Museum in Berlin, Germany (as of time of writing)

B Look at the infographic. Write where each of the objects are now. Then check (✓) the items that have already been returned to their countries of origin.

1. ☐ royal statues of Dahomey _____

2. ☐ cotton "ghost shirt" _____

3. ☐ bust of Nefertiti _____

4. ☐ stone moai statue _____

C 🎧 Listen to a conversation between two people. Answer the questions.

1. What are they debating?

_____

2. How are Sharon and Vic's perspectives different?

_____

_____

3. Who do you think convinced the other person more, and why?

_____

_____

COMMUNICATE *Synthesize and evaluate ideas*

D Work with a partner. Read Sharon's and Vic's opinions below. How much do you agree with them? Circle a number from from 1 (strongly disagree) to 5 (strongly agree). Do you think Jim Chuchu would agree with the opinions?

a. Museums shouldn't have to return legally-acquired objects.	1	2	3	4	5
b. Objects can still be cultural symbols wherever they're housed.	1	2	3	4	5
c. Countries benefit from the publicity foreign museums generate.	1	2	3	4	5
d. Historical artifacts serve as symbols of cultural pride and identity.	1	2	3	4	5
e. Cultural objects are better appreciated in their home countries.	1	2	3	4	5
f. Museums can replace original artifacts with identical copies.	1	2	3	4	5

E Work in a group. Come up with a list of criteria that museums around the world could use to decide which objects should be returned to their original countries.

> I think artifacts that were acquired illegally should definitely be returned.

> Absolutely! But who determines if the items were acquired illegally?

Putting It Together

ASSIGNMENT

Individual presentation: You are going to give a presentation on two items, practices, or traditions that are important symbols of a culture you appreciate.

PREPARE

A Review the unit. Find examples of things that can represent a culture.

_____

_____

_____

B Choose a culture you're interested in. Then use your ideas in Exercise A to help you brainstorm a few items, practices, or traditions that are important symbols of that culture.

_____

_____

_____

C Plan your presentation. Choose two items, practices, or traditions from Exercise B. Make notes in the chart.

What is it?		
What is its history?		
Why is it culturally significant?		
What does it teach us about the culture?		

D Look back at the vocabulary, pronunciation, and communication skills you've learned in this unit. What can you use in your presentation? Note any useful language below.

_____

_____

_____

_____

_____

E 🎧 Listen to an excerpt from Jim Chuchu's TED Talk. What words did he repeat? Why do you think he chose to repeat those words? Now look at your notes in Exercise C. Where can you use repetition to similar effect in your presentation?

F Practice your presentation. Make use of the presentation skill that you've learned.

PRESENT

G Give your presentation to a partner. Watch their presentation and evaluate them using the Presentation Scoring Rubrics at the back of the book.

H Discuss your evaluation with your partner. Give feedback on two things they did well and two areas for improvement.

Presentation Skill

Using Repetition as a Rhetorical Device

In his TED Talk, Jim Chuchu sometimes repeats key phrases to drive home ideas that he feels are important. For example, in one part of his talk, he starts three consecutive sentences with the phrase "It means that we forget ...". This is a rhetorical device often used in public speaking, called "the Rule of Three". It helps add weight and emotion to key points, and makes your words more memorable.

Checkpoint

Reflect on what you have learned. Check your progress.

I can ... ☐ understand and use words to talk about culturally important objects.

accessible	**acquire**	**artifact**	**campaign**	**discrimination**
feature	**house**	**initiative**	**restitution**	**rich**

☐ use forms of *acquire*, *campaign*, *discrimination*, *feature*, and *initiative*.

☐ watch and understand a talk about cultural restitution.

☐ use emphasis.

☐ interpret an infographic about culturally significant objects.

☐ synthesize and evaluate ideas about cultural restitution.

☐ use repetition as a rhetorical device.

☐ give a presentation on things that can represent a culture.

Independent Student Handbook

The Independent Student Handbook is a resource you can use during and after this course. It provides additional support for listening, speaking, note-taking, pronunciation, presentation, and vocabulary skills.

Students from Howard University, Washington D.C., the United States, celebrate their graduation.

LISTENING AND NOTE-TAKING

LISTENING STRATEGIES

Predicting

Speakers giving formal talks usually begin by introducing themselves and then introducing their topic. Listen carefully to the introduction of the topic and try to anticipate what you will hear.

Strategies:

- Use visual information including titles on the board, on slides, or in a PowerPoint presentation.
- Think about what you already know about the topic.
- Ask yourself questions that you think the speaker might answer, e.g., *What's the reason for A? How did B happen?*
- Listen for specific introduction phrases (see **Useful Phrases for Presenting**).

Listening for main ideas

It is often important to be able to tell the difference between a speaker's main ideas and supporting details.

Strategies:

- Listen carefully to the introduction. The main idea is often stated at the end of the introduction.
- Listen for rhetorical questions, or questions that the speaker asks and then answers. Often the answer is the main idea.
- Notice ideas that are repeated or rephrased. Repetition and rephrasing often signal main ideas (see **Useful Phrases for Presenting**).

Listening for details

Supporting details can be a name or a number, an example, or an explanation. When looking for a specific kind of information, it's useful to listen for words that are related to the information you need.

Strategies:

- Listen for specific phrases that introduce an example (see **Useful Phrases for Presenting**).
- Notice if an example comes after a general statement from the speaker or is leading into a general statement.
- Notice nouns that might signal causes/reasons (e.g., *factors, influences, causes, reasons*) or effects/results (e.g., *effects, results, outcomes, consequences*).
- Notice verbs that might signal causes/reasons (e.g., *contribute to, affect, influence, determine, produce, result in*) or effects/results (often these are passive, e.g., *is affected by*).
- Listen for specific phrases that introduce reasons/causes and effects/results (see **Useful Phrases for Presenting**).

Understanding the structure of the presentation

An organized speaker will use certain expressions to alert you to the important information that will follow. Notice signal words and phrases that tell you how the presentation is organized and the relationship between main ideas.

Introduction

A good introduction includes something like a thesis statement, which identifies the topic and gives an idea of how the lecture or presentation will be organized. Here are some expressions to listen for that indicate a speaker is introducing a topic (see also **Useful Phrases for Presenting**):

I'll be talking about …   *My topic is …*

There are basically two groups …   *There are three reasons …*

Body

In the body of the lecture, the speaker will usually expand upon the topic. The speaker will use phrases that tell you the order of events or subtopics and their relationship. Here are some expressions to listen for (see also **Useful Phrases for Presenting**):

The first/next/final (point) is …   *First/Next/Finally, let's look at …*

Another reason is …   *However, …*

Conclusion

In a conclusion, the speaker often summarizes what has been said and may discuss what it means, or make predictions or suggestions. Sometimes speakers ask a question to get the audience to think about the topic. Here are some expressions to listen for (see also **Useful Phrases for Presenting**):

In conclusion, …   *In summary, …*

As you can see …   *I/We would recommend …*

Understanding meaning from context

Speakers may use words that are new to you, or words that you may not fully understand. In these situations, you can guess the meaning by using the context or situation itself.

Strategies:

- Use context clues to guess the meaning of the word, then check if your guess makes sense. What does the speaker say before and after the unfamiliar word? What clues can help you guess the meaning of the word?
- Listen for words and phrases that signal a definition or explanation (see **Useful Phrases for Presenting**).

Recognizing a speaker's bias

It's important to know if a speaker is objective about the topic. Objective speakers do not express an opinion. Speakers who have a bias or strong feeling about the topic may express views that are subjective.

Strategies:

- Notice subjective adjectives, adverbs, and modals that the speaker uses (e.g., *ideal, horribly, should, shouldn't*). These suggest that the speaker has a bias.
- Listen to the speaker's tone. Do they sound excited, happy, or bored?
- When presenting another point of view on the topic, is that other point of view given much less time and attention by the speaker?
- Listen for words that signal opinions (see **Communication Strategies**).

NOTE-TAKING STRATEGIES

Taking notes is a personalized skill. It is important to develop a note-taking system that works well for you. However, there are some common strategies that you can use to improve your note-taking.

Before you listen

- Focus. Try to clear your mind before the speaker begins so you can pay attention. If possible, review previous notes or what you already know about the topic.

As you listen

Take notes by hand

Research suggests that taking notes by hand rather than on a laptop or tablet is more effective. Taking notes by hand requires you to summarize, rephrase, and synthesize the information. This helps you *encode* the information, or put it into a form that you can understand and remember.

Listen for signal words and phrases

Speakers often use signal words and phrases (see **Useful Phrases for Presenting**) to organize their ideas and indicate what they are going to talk about. Listening for signal words and phrases can help you decide what information to write down in your notes. For example:

Today we're going to talk about three alternative methods that are ecofriendly, fast, and efficient.

Condense (shorten) information

- As you listen, focus on the most important ideas. The speaker will usually repeat, define, explain, and/or give examples of these ideas. Take notes on these ideas.

    Speaker: *Worldwide, people are using and wasting huge amounts of plastic. For example, Americans throw away 35 million plastic bottles a year.*

    Notes: *Waste plastic, e.g., U.S. 35 mil plastic bottles/year*

- Don't write full sentences. Write only key words (nouns, verbs, adjectives), phrases, or short sentences.

    Full sentence: *The Maldives built a sea wall around the main island of Malé.*

    Notes: *Built sea wall—Malé*

- Leave out information that is unnecessary.

    Full sentence: *Van den Bercken fell in love with the music of Handel.*

    Notes: *VDB loves Handel*

- Write numbers and statistics (*35 mil; 91%*).

- Use abbreviations (*e.g., ft., min., yr*) and symbols (*=, ≠, >, <, %*).

- Use indenting. Write main ideas on the left side of the paper. Indent details.

    - *Benefits of car sharing*
        - *Save $*
            - *Saved $300-400/mo.*

- Write details under key terms to help you remember them.

- Write the definitions of important new words from the presentation.

After you listen

- Review your notes soon after the lecture or presentation. Add any details you missed.
- Clarify anything you don't understand in your notes with a classmate or teacher.
- Add or highlight main ideas. Cross out details that aren't important or necessary.
- Rewrite anything that is hard to read or understand. Rewrite your notes in an outline or other graphic organizer to record the information more clearly (see **Organizing Information**).
- Use arrows, boxes, diagrams, or other visual cues to show relationships between ideas.

Organizing information

Sometimes it is helpful to take notes using a graphic organizer. You can use one to take notes while you are listening or to organize your notes after you listen. Here are some examples of graphic organizers:

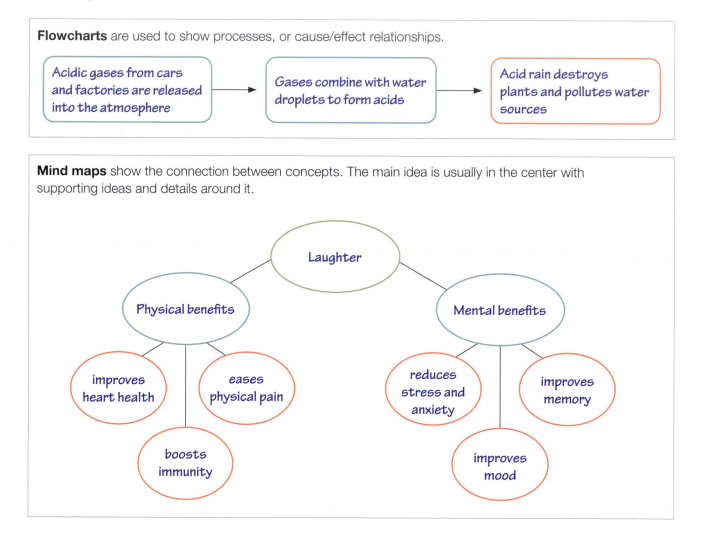

Flowcharts are used to show processes, or cause/effect relationships.

> Acidic gases from cars and factories are released into the atmosphere → Gases combine with water droplets to form acids → Acid rain destroys plants and pollutes water sources

Mind maps show the connection between concepts. The main idea is usually in the center with supporting ideas and details around it.

> Laughter
> - Physical benefits
>   - improves heart health
>   - eases physical pain
>   - boosts immunity
> - Mental benefits
>   - reduces stress and anxiety
>   - improves memory
>   - improves mood

Outlines show the relationship between main ideas and details.

To use an outline for taking notes, write the main ideas starting at the left margin of your paper. Below the main ideas, indent and write the supporting ideas and details. You can do this as you listen, or go back and rewrite your notes as an outline later.

1. Saving Water
   A. Why is it crucial to save water?
      i. Save money
      ii. Not enough fresh water in the world

T-charts compare two topics.

Hands-On Learning	
Advantages	**Disadvantages**
1. Uses all the senses (sight, touch, etc.)	1. Requires many types of materials
2. Encourages student participation	2. May be more difficult to manage large classes
3. Helps memory	3. Requires more teacher time to prepare

Timelines show a sequence of events.

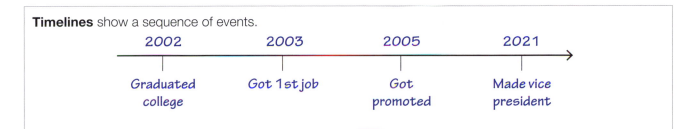

2002	2003	2005	2021
Graduated college	Got 1st job	Got promoted	Made vice president

Venn diagrams compare and contrast two or more topics. The overlapping areas show similarities.

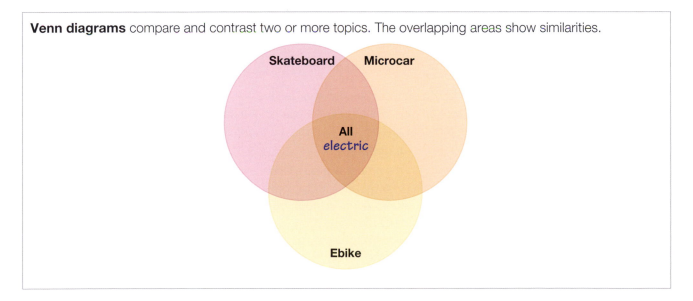

SPEAKING AND PRONUNCIATION

COMMUNICATION STRATEGIES

Successful communication requires cooperation from both the listener and speaker. In addition to verbal cues, the speaker can use gestures and other body language to convey their meaning. Similarly, the listener can use a range of verbal and non-verbal cues to show acknowledgment and interest, clarify meaning, and respond appropriately.

USEFUL PHRASES FOR EXPRESSING YOURSELF

The list below shows some common phrases for expressing ideas and opinions in class.

Expressing opinions

Your opinion is what you think or feel about something. You can add an adverb or adjective to make your statement stronger.

I think …	*If you ask me, …*
I feel …	*To me, …*
I'm sure …	*In my (honest) opinion/view …*
Personally, …	*I strongly believe …*

Expressing likes and dislikes

There are many expressions you can use to talk about your preferences other than *I like …* and *I don't like …* Using different expressions can help you sound less repetitive.

I enjoy …	*I can't stand …*
I prefer …	*I hate …*
I love …	*I really don't like …*
I don't mind …	*I don't care for …*

Giving facts

Using facts is a good and powerful way to support your ideas and opinions. Your listener will be more likely to believe and trust what you say.

There is evidence/proof …	*Researchers found …*
Experts claim/argue …	*The record shows …*
Studies show …	

Giving tips or suggestions

There are direct and indirect ways of giving suggestions. Imperatives are very direct and let your listener know that it's important they follow your advice. Using questions can make advice sound less direct—it encourages your listener to consider your suggestion.

Direct	Indirect
Imperatives (e.g., Try to get more sleep.*)*	*It's probably a good idea to …*
You/We should/shouldn't …	*How about + (noun/gerund)*
You/We ought to …	*What about + (noun/gerund)*
I suggest (that) …	*Why don't we/you …*
Let's …	*You/We could …*

USEFUL PHRASES FOR INTERACTING WITH OTHERS

The list below shows some common phrases for interacting with your classmates during pair and group work exercises.

Agreeing and disagreeing

In a discussion, you will often need to say whether you agree or disagree with the ideas or opinions shared. It's also good to give reasons for why you agree or disagree.

Agree		Disagree
I agree.	*Definitely.*	*I disagree.*
True.	*Right!*	*I'm not so sure about that.*
Good point.	*I was just about to say that.*	*I don't know.*
Exactly.		*That's a good point, but I don't really agree.*
Absolutely.		*I see what you mean, but I think that …*

Checking your understanding

To make sure that you understand what the speaker has said correctly, sometimes you might need to clarify what you hear. You can check your understanding by rephrasing what the speaker said or by asking for more information.

Are you saying that … ?	*How so?*
So what you mean is … ?	*I'm not sure I understand/follow.*
What do you mean?	*Do you mean … ?*
How's that?	*I'm not sure what you mean.*

Clarifying your meaning

When listeners need to clarify what they hear or understand, speakers need to respond appropriately. Speakers can restate their main points or directly state implied main points.

What I mean by that is …	*The point I'm making is that …*
Not at all.	

Checking others' understanding

When presenting information that is new to listeners, it's good to ask questions to make sure that your listeners have understood what you said.

Does that make sense?	*Is that clear?*
Do you understand?	*Are you following me?*
Do you see what I mean?	*Do you have any questions?*

Asking for opinions

When we give an opinion or suggestion, it's good to ask other people for theirs, too. Ask questions to show your desire to hear from your listeners and encourage them to share their views.

What do you think?	*How do you feel?*
Do you have anything to add?	*What's your opinion?*
What are your thoughts?	*We haven't heard from you in a while.*

Taking turns

During a presentation or discussion, sometimes a listener might want to interrupt the speaker to ask a question or share their opinion. Using questions is a polite way of interrupting. However, the speaker may choose not to allow the interruption, especially if they are about to finish what they have to say.

Interrupting	Stopping others from interrupting
Excuse me.	*Could I finish what I was saying?*
Pardon me.	*If you'd allow me to finish …*
Can I say something?	*Just one more thing.*
May I say something?	
Could I add something?	**Continuing with your presentation**
Can I just say … ?	*May I continue?*
Can I stop you for a second?	*Let me finish.*
Sorry to interrupt, but …	*Let's get back to …*

Asking for repetition

When a speaker speaks too fast or uses words that you are not familiar with, you might want the speaker to repeat themselves. You could apologize first, then politely ask the speaker to repeat what they said.

Could you say that again?	*I'm sorry. I missed that. What did you say?*
I'm sorry?	*Could you repeat that, please?*
I didn't catch what you said.	

Showing interest

It's polite to show interest when you're having a conversation with someone. You can show interest by asking questions or using certain words and phrases. You can also use body language like nodding your head or smiling.

I see.	*Seriously?*	*Wow.*
Good for you.	*Um-hmm.*	*And? (Then what?)*
Really?	*No kidding!*	*That's funny/amazing/incredible/awful!*

PRONUNCIATION STRATEGIES

When speaking English, it's important to pay attention to the pronunciation of specific sounds. It is also important to learn how to use rhythm, stress, and pausing. Below are some tips about English pronunciation.

Specific sounds

Research suggests that clear pronunciation of consonant sounds (as compared to vowel sounds) is a lot more useful in helping listeners understand speech. This means that consonant sounds must be accurate for your speech to be clear and easy to understand. For example, /m/ and /n/ are two sounds that sound similar. In a pair of words like *mail* and *nail*, it is important to pronounce the consonant clearly so that the listener knows which word you are referring to.

But there are some exceptions. One example is the pair /ð/ and /θ/, as in *other* and *thing*. These are very often pronounced (both by first and second language English users) as /d/ and /t/ or /v/ and /f/ with little or no impact on intelligibility. There is a lot of variation in vowel sounds in Englishes around the world; however, these differences rarely lead to miscommunication.

Vowels			**Consonants**		
Symbol	Key Word	Pronunciation	Symbol	Key Word	Pronunciation
/ɑ/	hot	/hɑt/	/b/	boy	/bɔɪ/
	far	/fɑr/	/d/	day	/deɪ/
/æ/	cat	/kæt/	/ʤ/	just	/ʤʌst/
/aɪ/	fine	/faɪn/	/f/	face	/feɪs/
/aʊ/	house	/haʊs/	/g/	get	/gɛt/
/ɛ/	bed	/bɛd/	/h/	hat	/hæt/
/eɪ/	name	/neɪm/	/k/	car	/kɑr/
/i/	need	/nid/	/l/	light	/laɪt/
/ɪ/	sit	/sɪt/	/m/	my	/maɪ/
/oʊ/	go	/goʊ/	/n/	nine	/naɪn/
/ʊ/	book	/bʊk/	/ŋ/	sing	/sɪŋ/
/u/	boot	/but/	/p/	pen	/pɛn/
/ɔ/	dog	/dɔg/	/r/	right	/raɪt/
	four	/fɔr/	/s/	see	/si/
/ɔɪ/	toy	/tɔɪ/	/t/	tea	/ti/
/ʌ/	cup	/kʌp/	/ʧ/	cheap	/ʧip/
/ɛr/	bird	/bɛrd/	/v/	vote	/voʊt/
/ə/	about	/əˈbaʊt/	/w/	west	/wɛst/
	after	/ˈæftər/	/j/	yes	/jɛs/
			/z/	zoo	/zu/
			/ð/	they	/ðeɪ/
			/θ/	think	/θɪŋk/
			/ʃ/	shoe	/ʃu/
			/ʒ/	vision	/ˈvɪʒən/

Source: *The Newbury House Dictionary plus Grammar Reference*, Fifth Edition, National Geographic Learning/Cengage Learning, 2014.

Rhythm

The rhythm of English involves stress and pausing.

Stress

- English words are based on syllables—units of sound that include one vowel sound.
- In every word in English, one syllable has the strongest stress.
- In English, speakers group words that go together based on the meaning and context of the sentence. These groups of words are called *thought groups*. In each thought group, one word is stressed more than the others—the stress is placed on the stressed syllable in this word.
- In general, new ideas and information are stressed.

Pausing

- Pauses in English can be divided into two groups: long and short pauses.
- English speakers use long pauses to mark the conclusion of a thought, items in a list, or choices given.
- Short pauses are used between thought groups to break up the ideas in sentences into smaller, more manageable chunks of information.

Intonation

English speakers use intonation, or pitch (the rise and fall of their voice), to help express meaning. For example, speakers usually use a rising intonation at the end of *yes/no* questions, and a falling intonation at the end of *wh-* questions and statements.

PRESENTING

PRESENTATION STRATEGIES

The strategies below will help you to prepare, present, and reflect on your presentations.

Prepare

As you prepare your presentation:

Consider your topic

- *Choose a topic you feel passionate about.* If you are passionate about your topic, your audience will be more interested and excited about your topic, too. Focus on one major idea that you can bring to life. The best ideas are the ones your audience wants to experience.

Consider your purpose

- *Have a strong beginning.* Use an effective *hook*, such as a quote, an interesting example, a rhetorical question, or a powerful image to get your audience's attention. Include one sentence that explains what you will do in your presentation and why.
- *Stay focused.* Make sure your details and examples support your main points. Avoid sidetracks or unnecessary information that takes you away from your topic.
- *Use visuals that relate to your ideas.* Drawings, photos, video clips, infographics, charts, maps, slides, and physical objects can get your audience's attention and explain ideas effectively, quickly, and clearly. Slides with only key words and phrases can help emphasize your main points. Visuals should be bright, clear, and simple.
- *Have a strong conclusion.* A strong conclusion should serve the same purpose as the strong beginning—to get your audience's attention and make them think. Good conclusions often refer back to the introduction, or beginning, of the presentation. For example, if you ask a question in the beginning, you can answer it in the conclusion. Remember to restate your main points, and add a conclusion device such as a question, a call to action, or a quote.

Consider your audience

- *Share a personal story.* You can also present information that will get an emotional reaction; for example, information that will make your audience feel surprised, curious, worried, or upset. This will help your audience relate to you and your topic.
- *Use familiar concepts.* Think about the people in your audience. Ask yourself these questions: Where are they from? How old are they? What is their background? What do they already know about my topic? What information do I need to explain? Use language and concepts they will understand.
- *Be authentic (be yourself).* Write your presentation yourself. Use words that you know and are comfortable using.

Rehearse

- *Make an outline.* This will help you organize your ideas.
- *Write notes on notecards.* Do not write full sentences, just key words and phrases to help you remember important ideas. Mark the words you should stress and places to pause.
- *Check the pronunciation of words.* Review the pronunciation skills in your book. For words that you are uncertain about, check with a classmate or a teacher, or look them up in a dictionary. Note and practice the pronunciation of difficult words.
- *Memorize the introduction and conclusion.* Rehearse your presentation several times. Practice saying it out loud to yourself (perhaps in front of a mirror or video recorder) and in front of others.
- *Ask for feedback.* Use feedback and your own performance in rehearsal to help you revise your material. If specific words or phrases are still a problem, rephrase them.

Present

As you present:

- Pay attention to your pacing (how fast or slow you speak). Remember to speak slowly and clearly. Pause to allow your audience to process information.

- Speak at a volume loud enough to be heard by everyone in the audience, but not too loud. Ask the audience if your volume is OK at the beginning of your talk.

- Vary your intonation. Don't speak in the same tone throughout the talk. Your audience will be more interested if your voice rises and falls, speeds up and slows down to match the ideas you are talking about.

- Be friendly and relaxed with your audience. Remember to smile!

- Show enthusiasm for your topic. Use humor if appropriate.

- Have a relaxed body posture. Don't stand with your arms folded or look down at your notes. Use gestures when helpful to emphasize your points.

- Don't read directly from your notes. Use them to help you remember ideas.

- Don't look at or read from your visuals too much. Use them to support and illustrate your ideas.

- Make frequent eye contact with the entire audience.

Reflect

As you reflect on your presentation:

- Consider what you think went well during your presentation and what areas you can improve on.

- Get feedback from your classmates and teacher. How do their comments relate to your own thoughts about your presentation? Did they notice things you didn't? How can you use their feedback in your next presentation?

USEFUL PHRASES FOR PRESENTING

The chart below provides some common signposts and signal words and phrases that speakers use in the introduction, body, and conclusion of a presentation.

INTRODUCTION	
Introducing a topic	
I'm going to talk about …	*So we're going to show you …*
My topic is …	*Now/Right/So/Well,* (pause) *let's look at …*
I'm going to present …	*There are three groups/reasons/effects/factors …*
I plan to discuss …	*There are four steps in this process.*
Let's start with …	
Today we're going to talk about …	

BODY	
Listing or sequencing	**Signaling problems/solutions**
First/First of all/The first (noun)*/To start/To begin, …*	*The problem/issue/challenge (with …) is …*
Second/Secondly/The second/Next/Another/Also/Then/In addition, …	*One solution/answer/response is …*
Last/The last/Finally …	
There are many/several/three types/kinds of/ways, …	

Giving reasons or causes

Because + (clause): Because it makes me feel happy …

Because of + (noun phrase): Because of climate change …

Due to + (noun phrase) …

Since + (clause) …

The reason that I like video games is …

One reason that people do surveys is …

One factor is + (noun phrase) …

The main reason that …

Giving results or effects

so + (clause): so I decided to try photography

Therefore, + (sentence): Therefore, I changed my diet.

As a result, + (sentence).

Consequently, + (sentence).

… causes + (noun phrase)

… leads to + (noun phrase)

… had an impact/effect on + (noun phrase)

If … then …

Giving examples

The first example is…

Here's an example of what I mean …

For instance, …

For example, …

Let me give you an example …

… such as …

… like …

Repeating and rephrasing

What you need to know is …

I'll say this again, …

So again, let me repeat …

The most important point is …

Signaling additional examples or ideas

Not only … but

Besides …

Not only do … but also

Signaling to stop taking notes

You don't need this for the test.

This information is in your books/on your handout/ on the website.

You don't have to write all this down.

Identifying a side track

This is off-topic, …

On a different subject, …

As an aside, …

That reminds me ….

Returning to a previous topic

Getting back to our previous discussion, …

To return to our earlier topic …

OK, getting back on topic …

So to return to what we were saying, …

Signaling a definition

Which means …

What that means is …

Or …

In other words, …

Another way to say that is …

That is …

That is to say …

Talking about visuals

This graph/infographic/diagram shows/explains …

The line/box/image represents …

The main point of this visual is …

You can see …

From this we can see …

CONCLUSION

Concluding

Well/So, that's how I see it.

In conclusion, …

In summary, …

To sum up, …

As you can see, …

At the end, …

To review, + (restatement of main points)

BUILDING VOCABULARY

VOCABULARY LEARNING STRATEGIES

Vocabulary learning is an ongoing process. The strategies below will help you learn and remember new vocabulary.

Guessing meaning from context

You can often guess the meaning of an unfamiliar word by looking at or listening to the words and sentences around it. Speakers usually know when a word is unfamiliar to the audience, or is essential to understanding the main ideas, and will often provide clues to its meaning.

- Restatement or synonyms: A speaker may give a synonym to explain the meaning of a word, using phrases such as *in other words, also called, or …,* and *also known as.*

- Antonyms: A speaker may define a word by explaining what it is NOT. The speaker might say *unlike A, …,* or *in contrast to A, B is …*

- Definitions: Listen for signals such as *which means* or *is defined as*. Definitions can also be signaled by a pause.

- Examples: A speaker may provide examples that can help you figure out what something is. For example, *Paris-Plage is a* **recreation** *area on the River Seine, in Paris, France. It has a sandy beach, a swimming pool, and areas for inline skating, playing volleyball, and other activities.*

Understanding word families: stems, prefixes, and suffixes

Use your understanding of stems, prefixes, and suffixes to recognize unfamiliar words and to expand your vocabulary. A stem is the root part of the word, which provides the main meaning.

A prefix is before the stem and usually modifies meaning (e.g., adding *re-* to a word means "again"). A suffix is after the stem and usually changes the part of speech (e.g., adding *-ation/-sion/-ion* to a verb changes it to a noun). For example, in the word *endangered*, the stem or root is *danger*, the prefix is *en-*, and the suffix is *-ed*. Words that share the same stem or root belong to the same word family (e.g., *event, eventful, uneventful, uneventfully*).

Word Stem	Meaning	Examples
ann (or *enn*)	year	anniversary, millennium
chron(o)	time	chronological, synchronize
flex (or *flect*)	bend	flexible, reflection
graph	draw, write	graphics, paragraph
lab	work	labor, collaborate
mob	move	mobility, automobile
sect	cut	sector, bisect
vac	empty	vacant, evacuate

Prefix	Meaning	Examples
auto-	self	automatic, autonomy
bi-	two	bilingual, bicycle
dis-	not, negation, remove	disappear, disadvantage
inter-	between	internet, international
mis-	bad, badly, incorrectly	misunderstand, misjudge
pre-	before	prehistoric, preheat
re-	again, back	repeat, return
trans-	across, beyond	transfer, translate

Suffix	Part of speech	Examples
-able (or *-ible*)	adjective	believable, impossible
-en	verb	lengthen, strengthen
-ful	adjective	beautiful, successful
-ize	verb	modernize, summarize
-ly	adverb; adjective	carefully, happily; friendly, lonely
-ment	noun	assignment, statement
-tion (or *-sion*)	noun	education, occasion
-wards	adverb	backwards, forwards

Using a dictionary

A dictionary is a useful tool to help you understand unfamiliar vocabulary you read or hear. Here are some tips for using a dictionary:

- When you see or hear a new word, try to guess its part of speech (noun, verb, adjective, etc.) and meaning, then look it up in a dictionary.

- Some words have multiple meanings. Look up a new word in the dictionary and try to choose the correct meaning for the context. Then see if it makes sense within the context.

- When you look up a word, look at all the definitions to see if there is a basic core meaning. This will help you understand the word when it is used in a different context. Also look at all the related words or words in the same family. This can help you expand your vocabulary. For example, the core meaning of *structure* involves something built or put together.

struc·ture /ˈstrʌktʃər/ *n.* **1** [C] a building of any kind: *A new structure is being built on the corner.* **2** [C] any architectural object of any kind: *The Eiffel Tower is a famous Parisian structure.* **3** [U] the way parts are put together or organized: *the structure of a song‖a business's structure*
—*v.* [T] **-tured, -turing, -tures** to put together or organize parts of s.t.: *We are structuring a plan to hire new teachers.* **-adj. structural.**

Source: *The Newbury House Dictionary plus Grammar Reference,* Fifth Edition, National Geographic Learning/Cengage Learning, 2014.

Multi-word units

You can improve your fluency if you learn and use vocabulary as multi-word units: idioms (*mend fences*), collocations (*trial and error*), and fixed expressions (*in other words*). Some multi-word units can only be understood as a chunk—the individual words do not add up to the same overall meaning. Keep track of multi-word units in a notebook or on note cards.

Collocations

A collocation is two or more words that often go together. A good way to sound more natural and fluent is to learn and remember as many collocations as you can. Look out for collocations as you read a new text or watch a presentation. Then note them down and try to use them when speaking or in your presentation.

You can organize your notes in a chart to make it easier to review and add to the list as you learn more collocations:

share an have an ask for change your	**opinion(s)**
fulfill manage set exceed	**expectation(s)**
encounter	problems resistance obstacles difficulty

Vocabulary note cards

You can expand your vocabulary by using vocabulary note cards. Write the word, expression, or sentence that you want to learn on one side. On the other, draw a four-square grid and write the following information in the squares: definition, translation (in your first language), sample sentence, synonyms. Choose words that are high frequency or on the academic word list. If you have looked a word up a few times, you should make a card for it.

definition:	*first language translation:*
sample sentence:	*synonyms:*

Organize the cards in review sets so you can practice them. Don't put words that are similar in spelling or meaning in the same review set, as you may get them mixed up. Go through the cards and test yourself on the meanings of the words or expressions. You can also practice with a partner.

Presentation Scoring Rubrics

Unit 1

Presenter(s): _____

The presenter(s) …

	Fair 🙂	Good 😁	Excellent! 🤩
started with an interesting question.			
presented information in a logical sequence that was easy to follow.			
spoke clearly with appropriate pacing, volume, and intonation.			
presented their survey findings clearly and precisely			
arrived at a meaningful conclusion based on their survey results.			
What did you like?	1. 2.		
What could be improved?	1. 2.		

Unit 2

Presenter(s): _____

The presenter(s) …

	Fair 🙂	Good 😁	Excellent! 🤩
presented information in a logical sequence that was easy to follow.			
spoke clearly with appropriate pacing, volume, and intonation.			
used visuals to make the presentation more interesting and engaging.			
explained multiple benefits of the recommended habit.			
spoke persuasively and convincingly.			
What did you like?	1. 2.		
What could be improved?	1. 2.		

Unit 3

Presenter(s): _____

The presenter(s) …

	Fair 🙂	Good 😁	Excellent! 🤩
presented information in a logical sequence that was easy to follow.			
spoke clearly with appropriate pacing, volume, and intonation.			
used gestures to make the presentation more engaging.			
defined the problems and causes clearly and precisely.			
explained how listening more would help solve the problems.			
What did you like?	1. 2.		
What could be improved?	1. 2.		

Unit 4

Presenter(s): _____

The presenter(s) …

	Fair 🙂	Good 😁	Excellent! 🤩
presented information in a logical sequence that was easy to follow.			
spoke clearly with appropriate pacing, volume, and intonation.			
chose suitable anecdotes to explain the pros and cons of risk-taking.			
added details to make their anecdotes descriptive, interesting, and relatable.			
ended the presentation with a meaningful conclusion.			
What did you like?	1. 2.		
What could be improved?	1. 2.		

Unit 5

Presenter(s): _____

The presenter(s) …

	Fair 🙂	Good 😄	Excellent! 🤩
presented information in a logical sequence that was easy to follow.			
spoke clearly with appropriate pacing, volume, and intonation.			
considered their audience and made the presentation relatable to them.			
explained the solution, its benefits and its challenges.			
compared the solution with alternatives			

What did you like?	1. 2.
What could be improved?	1. 2.

Unit 6

Presenter(s): _____

The presenter(s) …

	Fair 🙂	Good 😄	Excellent! 🤩
presented information in a logical sequence that was easy to follow.			
spoke clearly with appropriate pacing, volume, and intonation.			
provided interesting context when talking about their photos.			
explained clearly why the photos were or were not meaningful.			
drew clear conclusions about when taking photos and videos is worthwhile.			

What did you like?	1. 2.
What could be improved?	1. 2.

Unit 7

Presenter(s): _____

The presenter(s) …

	Fair 😊	Good 😁	Excellent! 🤩
presented information in a logical sequence that was easy to follow.			
spoke clearly with appropriate pacing, volume, and intonation.			
identified and justified features of the ideal workplace			
explained how different generations would probably react to these ideas.			
used different techniques to make their presentation dynamic.			
What did you like?	1. 2.		
What could be improved?	1. 2.		

Unit 8

Presenter(s): _____

The presenter(s) …

	Fair 😊	Good 😁	Excellent! 🤩
presented information in a logical sequence that was easy to follow.			
spoke clearly with appropriate pacing, volume, and intonation.			
explained the cultural significance of the things they chose.			
used repetition to add weight and emotion to key points.			
included a meaningful conclusion about the importance of cultural symbols.			
What did you like?	1. 2.		
What could be improved?	1. 2.		

Vocabulary Index

Word	Unit	CEFR	Word	Unit	CEFR	Word	Unit	CEFR
accessible*	U8	B2	expression	U2	B2	one-on-one	U3	C1
acknowledge*	U3	B2	extract*	U5	B2	optimism	U7	C1
acquire*	U8	B2	facilitate*	U3	C1	originate	U8	C1
adapt*	U4	B2	fake	U1	B2	outcome*	U4	C1
addiction	U6	B2	fatigued	U2	C1	outlook	U7	C1
adjustment*	U2	B2	feature*	U8	B2	overtake	U7	B2
adopt	U2	B2	feedback	U3	B2	passion	U3	B2
adversely	U6	C1	flexibility*	U7	B2	patronizing	U3	C2
agriculture	U5	B2	flourish	U5	C1	perception*	U3	C1
aid*	U3	C1	frown	U2	C1	persevere	U2	C1
alleviate	U5	C1	frustrated	U7	C1	perspective*	U6	C1
anecdote	U1	C1	fulfil	U2	B2	phenomenon*	U4	C1
appropriate*	U7	B2	gadget	U6	C1	pragmatic	U7	C2
artifact	U8	C2	genuine	U8	B2	pressure	U7	B2
aversion	U4	C2	globalization*	U8	C1	probability	U4	C1
bias*	U4	B2	grasp	U3	C1	prone to	U4	C2
breakthrough	U5	B2	guarantee*	U4	B2	proximity	U6	C2
campaign	U8	C1	harvest	U5	B2	radically*	U7	C1
cellular	U5	C1	house	U8	C2	rational*	U4	C1
characterize	U7	C1	housing	U7	C1	rear	U5	C1
circumstance*	U7	B2	idealistic	U7	C1	reckless	U4	C1
client	U3	B2	imitate	U1	C1	rejection*	U8	C1
committed*	U6	B2	impulse	U6	C2	relief	U6	B2
compelling	U6	C1	inappropriate*	U8	C1	resource*	U3	B2
confusion	U3	B2	incorporate*	U2	C2	restitution	U8	C2
consequence*	U4	B2	induce*	U2	C1	restore*	U5	B2
consideration	U8	B2	ingenuity	U5	C2	rich	U8	B2
consistency*	U2	C1	initiate*	U3	C1	sensational	U1	C1
consume*	U5	B2	initiative*	U8	C1	shape	U1	B2
controversial*	U8	B2	interaction*	U3	C1	solely*	U6	C1
cooperation*	U3	B2	interpretation*	U3	C1	source*	U1	B2
coverage	U1	C1	intuition	U4	C2	stable*	U5	C1
daring	U4	B2	journalism	U1	B2	staple	U5	C2
debt	U7	B2	label*	U8	B1	statistic*	U1	C1
deficiency	U5	C1	landmark	U6	C1	stereotype	U7	C1
detect*	U1	C1	lifestyle	U2	B2	subjective	U3	C1
determine	U2	C1	limitation	U6	C1	subscription	U1	C1
diminish*	U6	C1	livestock	U5	C1	suffering	U5	B2
discipline	U2	B2	long-lasting	U2	C2	suppress	U2	C1
discrimination*	U8	C1	mature*	U4	B2	swap	U2	C1
disproportionate*	U1	C2	medium*	U1	B2	texture	U1	C1
disrespect	U8	C1	mental*	U4	B2	trait	U7	C2
distort*	U1	C1	mimic	U2	B2	transcend	U6	C1
donor	U3	C1	misrepresent	U1	C1	transformation*	U5	C1
edible	U5	C1	misunderstand	U7	B2	unforeseen	U4	C1
emotional	U2	B2	misuse	U1	C1	value	U7	C1
empower	U6	C1	modify*	U2	C1	verify	U1	C1
enhance*	U1	C1	negligent	U1	C2	versatile	U6	C2
enterprise	U3	C1	nuanced	U6	C2	vulnerable	U4	C1
entitled	U7	C1	nutrition	U5	C1	well-being	U2	C1
equivalent*	U5	C1	objective*	U3	B2	widespread*	U6	B2
escalate	U4	C1	obligation	U6	B2	workforce	U7	C1
exceptionally	U4	C1	odds*	U4	C1			
excessive	U6	C1	offend	U8	B2			

These words are on the Academic Word List (AWL). The AWL is a list of the 570 most frequent word families in academic texts. It does not include the most frequent 2,000 words of English.

Credits

Acknowledgments

The authors and publisher would like to thank the following teachers from all over the world for their valuable input during the development process of *21st Century Communication*, Second Edition.

Adriana Baiardi, Colegio Fatima; **Anouchka Rachelson**, Miami Dade College; **Ariya Kilpatrick**, Bellevue College; **Beth Steinbach**, Austin Community College; **Bill Hodges**, University of Guelph; **Carl Vollmer**, Ritsumeikan Uji Junior and Senior High School; **Carol Chan**, National TsingHua University; **Dalit Berkowitz**, Los Angeles City College; **David A. Isaacs**, Hokuriku University; **David Goodman**, National Kaohsiung University of Hospitality and Tourism; **Diana Ord**, Emily Griffith Technical School; **Elizabeth Rodacker**, Bakersfield College; **Emily Brown**, Hillsborough Community College; **Erin Frederickson**, Macomb Community College; **George Rowe**, Bellevue College; **Heba Elhadary**, Gulf University for Science and Technology; **Kaoru Lisa Silverman**, Kyushu Sangyo University; **Lu-Chun Lin**, National Yang Ming Chiao Tung University; **Madison Griffin**, American River College; **Mahmoud Salman**, Global Bilingual Academy; **Marta O. Dmytrenko-Ahrabian**, Wayne State University; **Michael G. Klüg**, Wayne State University; **Monica Courtney**, LaGuardia Community College; **Nora Frisch**, Truckee Meadows Community College; **Pamela Smart-Smith**, Virginia Tech; **Paula González y González**, Colegio Mar del Plata Day School; **Richard Alishio**, North Seattle College; **Rocío Tanzola**, Words; **Shaoyun Ma**, National TsingHua University; **Sorrell Yue**, Fukuoka University; **Susumu Onodera**, Hirosaki University; **Xinyue Hu**, Chongqing No. 2 Foreign Language School; **Yi Shan Tsai**, Golden Apple Language Institute; **Yohei Murayama**, Kagoshima University